978.1 M664e   M
MINER
THE END OF INDIAN KANSAS
                    12.50

WITHDRAWN

THE END OF INDIAN KANSAS

A Study of Cultural Revolution, 1854-1871

H. CRAIG MINER
and
WILLIAM E. UNRAU

THE REGENTS PRESS OF KANSAS
Lawrence

© Copyright 1978 by The Regents Press of Kansas
Printed in the United States of America
Designed by Yvonne Willingham

Library of Congress Cataloging in Publication Data

Miner, H   Craig.
    The end of Indian Kansas.

    Bibliography: p.
    Includes index.
    1. Indians of North America—Kansas—History.
2. Indians of North America—Kansas—Land tenure.
3. Indians of North America—Government relations.
4. Kansas—History. I. Unrau, William E., 1929-
joint author. II. Title.
E78.K16M56   978.1'004'97   77-4410
ISBN 0-7006-0161-9

Contents

List of Illustrations

Preface

NO HISTORY IS ALL THINGS to all people. Given the diversity of human experience and human expectation, it cannot and perhaps should not be otherwise. This book has as its objective the breaking of new ground by dealing with subjects and sources largely untreated in the published litterature on the American Indian. In the authors' opinion a vital flaw in the sweeping generalizations that have been made concerning the Indian policy of the United States in the nineteenth century is that they are too often based on how twentieth-century America would like to feel and think, and too seldom on careful examination of the voluminous documentary remains of that policy.

To be sure, there is no lack of published evidence that something went drastically wrong and that the Indians were treated unfairly. But is this all that we need to know? Can we afford to be largely ignorant of the personalities involved, the complex devices deployed, and the objectives pursued in the forced removal of thousands of Indians from Kansas? Can we continue to ignore the evidence, simply because the reiteration of traditional accounts seems sufficient? Too often it is forgotten that between 1854 and 1871 there was accomplished a second major removal of Indians in America, and yet, by comparison to the first—the one inaugurated during the Jacksonian era—virtually nothing from a serious, documentary point of view is known about it. To stereotype federal Indian policy and Indian-white relations of the nineteenth century based on a surface knowledge of the events is no more responsible than generalizing about the habits of the Choctaws from a study of the Oglallah Sioux. Kansas, which became a United States territory when not one square foot of it was legally available for public ownership, presents a complex and unusual case. Yet its pattern affected more Indians and occupied more government time than the celebrated exploits of the military against the more warlike western tribes—a hackneyed theme that has prompted whole volumes on single campaigns.

The focus of our presentation is topical. We have attempted to identify significant techniques by which the removal of Indians from Kansas was accomplished, and to show how the territory evolved from a so-called permanent habitat of thousands of Indians from formerly eastern tribes in 1854 to a state with only a few Kickapoos, Sacs and Foxes, Prairie Potawatomis, and assorted mixed-bloods by 1875. Because the tragic experiences of the Indians roaming through western Kansas—Southern Cheyennes and Arapahoes, Kiowas, Comanches, Plains Apaches, Pawnees, and Wichitas—followed different patterns of removal that have been well documented by other historians, and because these patterns did not seriously involve the various techniques of individual land tenure, timber and town-site speculation, and forced detribalization until the Plains Indians were permanently confined to future Oklahoma in the late 1870s, we have dealt with these tribes only as their experiences impinged upon the removal of the Indians from eastern Kansas. Once the business of removing the tribes in the eastern part of the state was accomplished, a quick series of military actions and the destruction of the bison supply were all that was necessary to bring the western tribes to reserves in Indian Territory. At all times our purpose has been to underscore the remarkable incongruities in Indian policy, land policy, law, and administration; and to indicate in detail the manner in which these conflicts were exploited by methods calculated to force the Indian from Kansas as rapidly as possible and, worse, to obliterate his traditional culture.

We hope the reader will understand that we are advocates of neither the red nor the white race but rather of humanity, in the largest sense, and of the historical axiom that revolutionary cultural change involves a complicated mix of good and sinister intentions on the part of both factions. After all, civilization vis-à-vis barbarism is a concept peculiar to the social scientist, not the historian. Yet because events never take place in a vacuum, and because we refuse to dissociate ourselves from time and place, we have made judgments when the evidence was overwhelming.

That the change from aboriginal dominance to proto-industrial civilization within a time span of twenty years presents a cultural revolution seems clear. It is our conviction that our study of the structure and methods of this nineteenth-century revolution applies to, and perhaps even predicts, the course of events in other instances where technologically advanced cultures attempt to deal with underdeveloped aboriginal groups who by historical accident and unforeseen circumstances possess valuable natural resources that must be exploited. We have attempted to outline not only actions but possible alternatives, and to call attention to ideas brought forward at the time which failed of acceptance for reasons largely unrelated to the good sense of the participants. In doing so we have attempted to give our readers a better understanding of the dynamics of cultural confrontation—the kind experienced by the Wyandot Indians, who, after a sojourn in Kansas, were able only to note that they were rich when the white man came and were poor and subject to removal when he had revealed his true purpose. They had been, they said, simply "unequal to the new and extraordinary state of things." With the hope that the student of Indian history may be somewhat more aware of extraordinary things, both then and now, we undertake to examine the end of Indian Kansas.

Acknowledgments

DURING THE COURSE OF RESEARCH undertaken for this study the authors enjoyed the professional assistance of the following persons: Richard Crawford and Robert M. Kvasnicka of the National Archives; Reid Whitaker of the Federal Records Center in Kansas City; George Yonkin, formerly of the Federal Records Center in Fort Worth; Rella Looney of the Oklahoma Historical Society; Joseph Snell and Eugene Decker of the Kansas State Historical Society; Russell E. Dybdahl, Thoburn Taggert, Jr., and Michael Heaston of Ablah Library, Wichita State University; Carl N. Tyson of Oklahoma State University; Joseph Gambone, Topeka, Kansas; Steve Day, Norman, Oklahoma; and Howard Bell, Riverside, California.

The authors also wish to acknowledge the financial support provided by the Faculty Research Committee, Wichita State University.

CHAPTER ONE

Territorial Kansas and the Indian

FROM THE JEFFERSONIAN ERA to the closing years of the nineteenth century the establishment of territories and states was considered a vital factor in the preservation and growth of American democracy. Frugal, hard-working farmers, so the argument had it, would turn the wilderness into a garden and in the process experience the sublime pleasures of egalitarianism. Nature in all her glory would respond to the man with the plow and bear witness to the divine character of the universe. Such was the persuasion. The reality was otherwise. Politicians debated the use of the public lands as a means of producing revenue as opposed to distributing it in fee simple to the venturesome, while land brokers, squatters, and special interest groups compromised their identification with the public interest and pursued a course calculated to enhance their own economic power. This course was indicative of America in the process of becoming. Kansas Territory in the decade following the Mexican War presented unusual opportunities for those accustomed to exploitation and appropriation of the public lands for their own purposes.

Formally organized on May 30, 1854, Kansas Territory extended more than six hundred miles west of Missouri—a vast region that was once considered a desert wasteland but which by the mid-nineteenth century was being viewed in a more favorable light. Moisture for traditional agricultural operations was more than sufficient on the eastern fringe; hardwood timber, essential to frontier self-sufficiency and quick profits, was in adequate supply in the same area. Farther west were bountiful grazing lands and what proved to be incredibly fertile prairies. While the High Plains west of the one-hundredth meridian awaited the soil scientist of the twentieth century for profitable development, it was only four years before a major gold strike near the western boundary acted as a magnet for hordes of "fifty-niners" to rush across the territory, observe its massive Indian population, and confirm its potential for white settlement.

As it is today, Kansas was then a land of extremes. Periodic droughts and other violent fluctuations in the weather made farming a hazardous enterprise, as did absentee ownership and control of the resources essential for economic development. To aggravate the situation, oversimplified beliefs in the virtues of evangelical Christianity in its assumed relationship to democratic fulfillment were frustrated by the more earthly behavior of charlatans deficient in moral performance. Differences in political ideology too often became irreconcilable and led to senseless acts of violence, especially as the expansion of chattel slavery into the trans-Missouri West became an ever more pressing issue. In short, Kansas at midcentury was a moral testing ground, and, as a number of scholars have already demonstrated, there is no better example of America experiencing a failure of institutional nerve than that afforded by the slave interests, free-soil partisans, squatters of uncertain ideology, speculators, and bureaucrats who confronted one another in Kansas Territory in the period immediately preceding the Civil War.[1]

But if the invaders of Kansas Territory faced one problem above all the rest in terms of its immediacy and intransigency, it was Indians—those troublesome Native Americans who seemed to retreat in response to the white man's advance, only to regroup and once again appear on the horizon. While an occasional voice of objection was raised among the invaders, the Indians' cultural inferiority was never seriously questioned. Indeed, only when the natives' actions departed from the conceptual framework imposed on them by the invaders were momentary concessions made—concessions, it should be emphasized, that often provided the means and legal instruments for future exploitation. And it was thus from the start. As Paul Wallace Gates so succinctly noted more than two decades ago, the main feature of the "Kansas struggle" was the opening of the territory to white settlement when not one acre of land was legally available to sell, and at a time when "there was emerging one of the most complex and confusing arrays of policies affecting the distribution of the public lands and the transfer to white ownership of Indian land-rights that have emerged in the continental United States, save perhaps Oklahoma." Gates characterized the ensuing struggle as one involving not just the slave issue —the classic "Bleeding Kansas" theme—but the more significant relationships between an inconsistent land system and what he termed the "many variations of plunder and political patronage" the anomalous situation prompted.[2]

While Gates' primary focus was on land disposal he nevertheless did much to dispel the notion that Indian removal from Kansas was largely a battlefield encounter between befeathered warriors on the one hand and hardy pioneers on the other. More than ten thousand Kickapoos, Delawares, Sacs and Foxes, Shawnees, Potawatomis, Kansas, Ottawas, Wyandots, Miamis, Osages—not to mention a number of smaller tribes—confined to arbitrarily determined reserves on the eastern border of the territory presented a far greater challenge to white settlement than the celebrated warriors of the Great Plains. To be sure, the struggle for the next two decades was not as spectatular as violence-conditioned America has come to expect at the cinema and on television. But the stakes were much larger, and, more importantly, those involved at the time knew it. This point can hardly be overemphasized. In retrospect it seems clear that the end of Indian Kansas and the obliteration of diverse

Indian cultures were virtually assured the moment a group of fumbling, short-sighted politicians opened the door to white settlement in 1854, and that all that was left was to work out the details—in Washington cloakrooms, in corporate boardrooms, in the so-called halls of justice, at potential town sites and railroad centers, and on the fertile, timbered Indian reserves that all assumed were the measure of progress. As a correspondent for a New York paper put it during the initial stages of the confrontation,

> It required no spirit of divination to foresee that, in opening the territory to a white population, the semi-barbarous occupancy of the finest lands by the Indians would inevitably terminate in some manner. I do not know whether the originators of the Kansas-Nebraska Bill contemplated an amalgamation of whites and Indians, to vindicate the faith of treaties and the progress of American civilization westward. If so, it was [a] blunder. Some few of the more intelligent and industrious Indians may be absorbed in the population of Kansas, but the great mass can neither use nor be used by civilization.

His certainty in the matter was questioned, albeit not very effectively, by a writer in the nation's capital whose analysis illustrates the confusion involved. To understand what was happening in Kansas Territory was "about as easy as it would have been to unravel the knot of the Phrygian or the riddle of the Sphinx; so we very early gave up the study in despair. All that we could discern with any distinctness," he concluded, "was the presence of unreasonable passions, selfish party aims, and unnatural prejudice."[3]

Expressions of this sort obviously were prompted by the slave controversy only recently fanned into a blaze by the Kansas-Nebraska Bill. At stake, however, was more than the future of the black man in the trans-Missouri West. While not immediately perceived in all its ramifications, the newly created Kansas Territory was firm evidence that the government's Indian policy dating back to the days of Jefferson,

Monroe, Calhoun, and Jackson was a dead letter. Beginning with the Shawnee treaty of December 30, 1825, and culminating in the Sac and Fox treaty of March 23, 1843, the eastern tribes had been assured that their trek to a distant region called Kansas was their final move. They had been encouraged to believe that the region west of Missouri was permanent Indian country, a place where the corrupting influences of the white man's culture would be excluded. Assuming that the Indians had an intense sense of national feeling, the Reverend Isaac McCoy, a Baptist dignitary and principal architect of the new dispensation, had insisted that the suffering tribes needed a land of their own, where under government supervision they might "feel their importance, where they [could] hope to enjoy, unmolested, the fruits of their labours, and [where] their national recovery need not be doubted." Indian country would remain a formal part of the United States, first in a colonial relationship and perhaps later as a state. In any case it would engross the more "enlightened" characteristics of the American nation and allow the government to relinquish once and for all its paternalistic responsibilities for the tribes. By 1854, however, such lofty theorizing had lost its appeal. Land was land, and the key to progress. It was the birthright of the man with the plow, and so long as it was defined as a public commodity it was open to exploitation, regardless of the consequences. Not even the paucity of white population in existing states and territories could make a difference, as Representative James Meacham learned only too well during the debates over the Kansas-Nebraska Bill. Citing Missouri, with only 10 persons per square mile, Iowa with only 3, Oregon with only .03, Minnesota with only .07, and New Mexico with only .28, the Vermont congressman insisted there was no need to open another "safety-valve" for foot-loose Americans. But the final vote on the bill proved that his words had fallen on deaf ears. Virgin soil, railroad rights of way, and lucrative town sites were more important than stuffy statistics and a permanent Indian policy conceived by a previous generation.[4]

A warning that the fires of removal had not gone out

was issued as early as March 3, 1853, when a rider attached to an otherwise routine Indian appropriation bill authorized the president "to enter into negotiations with Indian tribes west of the states of Missouri and Iowa for the purpose of securing the assent of said tribes to the settlement of the citizens of the United States upon lands claimed by said Indians, and for the purpose of extinguishing the title of said Indians in *whole* [italics added] or in part to said lands." Fuel was added to the fire by Thomas Hart Benton, former senator and indefatigable champion of frontier expansion and a trunk railroad to the Pacific that would benefit his native state of Missouri. His problem, of course, was that the most direct route to California was blocked by the emigrant reserves; but persistent examination of the alternatives revealed that the removal program inaugurated three decades earlier contained a fundamental flaw that might be exploited. To make room for more than ten thousand eastern Indians the government had been obliged to negotiate land cession treaties with the Kansas and Osages in 1825, and with the Pawnees in 1833. Perhaps with an eye to the future and the removal of even more Indians to a proposed Indian state, larger cessions had been obtained than were immediately needed, with the result that substantial tracts of the Neosho, Arkansas, and Smoky Hill river valleys were left unassigned and unoccupied. These lands, while neither strategic nor immediately attractive to white settlers (although extremely important to the bison culture of the Plains Indians), were seized upon by Benton and his associates and used as a mighty wedge to break the reservation log-jam on the western border of Missouri.[5]

Who were Benton's associates? The champions of popular sovereignty on both sides of the fence, those who saw Kansas Territory as the testing ground for the moral issue of the century, the arena for economic advancement, or, perhaps, the place where political careers at the infant stage might develop into maturity? To be sure, but a consideration of the realities suggests there were still others. In our own time they would be designated "Uncle Tomahawks"—that is, Indians (often mixed-bloods) whose partial acculturation into the mainstream of white life prompted them to pursue economic opportunities presented by the conflict between the races, while sustaining positions of influence within their traditional cultures. A case in point is Abelard Guthrie, mixed-blood Shawnee-Wyandot, whose opportunism complemented that of Benton. Like Tauy Jones of the Ottawas, Moses Keokuk of the Sacs and Foxes, and Paschal Fish of the Shawnees, Guthrie shifted ground as it suited his purpose. In 1854, for example, he abandoned the Wyandots and made an unsuccessful attempt to rejoin the Shawnees in order to secure a financial settlement he hoped the government would pay his mother. As an intractable abolitionist Guthrie played a major (although premature) role in the creation of Nebraska Territory. He was an enterprising spokesman against local and state taxation of Indian land and, in the late 1860s, was lobbying in Washington to secure passage of a private bill that had as its objective the granting to him personally 50 percent of all back debts the government owed the Shawnees and Wyandots. In short, Guthrie was a man of many faces—but always wearing the mask of an Indian— and, like Benton, he was interested in the main chance. Perhaps no better tribute to this mixed-blood's character and contribution to the end of Indian Kansas can be offered than that of an unidentified clerk in the Interior Department, who, shortly after Guthrie's death, recalled, "Poor Guthrie has gone to a higher tribunal where he will get justice."[6]

The relationship between Benton and Guthrie hinged on a map allegedly prepared by a Mr. Eastin in 1853. It was drawn in such a manner as to indicate that vast quantities of land in the proposed Kansas-Nebraska Territory were unassigned to Indians and thus open to squatter penetration. There is good evidence that the map may have been conceived and drawn under Guthrie's direction, based on his intricate knowledge of the process whereby the Wyandots had acquired their Kansas reservation, and that Eastin was only a pawn in the unfolding plan. In any case, by failing to display the legal boundaries of the emigrant reserves carved out of the Osage, Kansa, and Pawnee cessions of an earlier period, and then obtaining the sanction of Commissioner George Manypenny, who was asked to outline and certify only the *total* area reassigned to the eastern Indians, not the *individual* boundaries, the impression was given that massive quantities of unassigned land immediately west of Missouri were open to the squatters. While the misleading map was being widely distributed in the summer of 1853, Benton released a public statement emphasizing that because no limitation to settlement had been specifically mentioned in the law annexing the Indian country to Missouri for judicial purposes, there was no legal obstacle to the squatters. True, Benton admitted, the federal statute of 1807 had prohibited white encroachment on unassigned lands of the public domain, but it had in effect been obliterated by the Trade and Intercourse Act of 1834, for the simple reason that here was the first official definition of an area vaguely designated Indian country. Thus, by clever legalisms and an obscure solicitation from a too-trusting Indian commissioner, Benton and Guthrie had invited the spoliation of the emigrant reserves nearly a year before the establishment of Kansas Territory.[7]

Meanwhile, Manypenny had been dispatched to Indian country to feel out tribal leaders regarding cession treaties contemplated by the promoters of political organization west of Missouri. It was there, in early September, 1853, that Manypenny fully perceived the damaging character of the map. He was furious and, in an open letter to the public, charged that the publisher had done the Indian Office a profound disservice. Included with his letter was a copy of Benton's misleading instructions. Though Manypenny was well intentioned and wholly candid, his efforts nevertheless were styled the response of a petty bureaucrat; as a St. Louis paper was quick to retort, "The Mormons now settle on what Indian lands they please, driving off Indians and killing them . . . and all this upon Indian land to which the Indian title was never extinguished." Johnston Lykins, a Baptist minister supposedly dedicated to promoting civilization among the Indians west of Missouri, joined in the anti-Manypenny crusade. "It is true that some of the territory is still owned by the Indians," he admitted, but this in no way was to be considered an obstacle to white settlement of the lush Osage and upper Neosho valleys of Kansas. Other complaints were voiced regarding the commissioner's delaying tactics in securing the "right kind of treaties," but in the final analysis it was mixed-blood Guthrie who assumed a leadership role. Chastising Manypenny for not having attempted to negotiate a treaty that might clear the air, the sometime Wyandot and sometime Shawnee complained, "This Commissioner (my pen refuses to write the name of this reptile, than which natural history, with its long catalogue of vermin, has nothing more filthy) also made it known that he had given orders to the commanding officer at Fort Leavenworth to remove all white men from the public lands. Now where is the law investing the Commissioner with such powers? Is this fellow insane?"[8]

Commenting on Manypenny's trip to Kansas, a Washington paper stated, "The commissioner found the state of feeling on the frontier . . . somewhat excited, but before he left the territory the excitement was apparently quieted, and a very general readiness shown by the people to await patiently the action of the government." The fact is that Manypenny was caught between his naïve belief that the future of the emigrant tribes in Kansas rested on their accepting fee-simple land allotments on the model of the invading white farmers and the strategy of the Benton-Guthrie crowd, who viewed cession treaties as the first step in the inevitable process that would ultimately force all Indians to be removed from Kansas.[9]

A key to understanding the relative ease with which Benton and Guthrie were able to characterize Manypenny as an obstacle to progress—as well as a tool of the southern slavocracy, an enemy of railroad expansion, and an unreasonable champion of the Indian—was the success they experienced in identifying him with David Rice Atchison, Benton's antagonist and colleague in the Senate from Missouri. Atchison was determined to prevent Kansas from becoming a free-soil territory, and he saw the Indian question as the one most effective means whereby he might counteract the influence of Benton. Thus the Indians were forced to assume the role of pawns in the larger struggle over slavery and western economic development in general. Commenting on the alleged Atchison-Manypenny combination after the commissioner had returned to Washington without the acceptable land cession treaties, the pro-Benton *Missouri Democrat* charged, "It is known that Atchison's *tool,* Manypenny, violated the [1853] Act of Congress for holding treaties with our Western border Indians to prevent the extinction of titles, to delay the central [rail]road, and that he would do nothing until Benton put a 'coal fire' on his back." Earlier, the same paper accused Atchison of opposing cessions treaties for no other reason than to see the Indian country west of Missouri "sunk in hell, before it shall become a free-soil territory." Atchison fought back by insisting that the Osage, Kansa, and Pawnee treaties had been for "locating other Indians; that it was by both parties so understood, and not for the purpose of settling white men. I also deny," he continued, "that any person can under any law of Congress obtain a preemption right by settling on any [Kansas] land, and I deny that Col. Benton's map proves anything for him." Manypenny joined in by citing the Trade and Intercourse Act of 1834 which empowered the president to use military force if necessary to remove intruders from Indian country; he also emphasized that the Indian title to unassigned lands was good and that, until new treaties provided otherwise, the Indian claim to the country west of Missouri was absolute.[10]

For political reasons, however, Atchison found it necessary to endorse the Pacific railroad, with the result that Manypenny's defense of the tribes was compromised. "They all fought from behind the Indians, as if every territory in the Union had not been constituted before there had been extinction of the Indian title," smugly observed the Bentonites. "It was all a pretext, and a silly one." Under such circumstances, then, it should occasion no surprise that the debates over the Kansas-Nebraska Bill only amplified and clouded the Indian issue by attaching it to the issues of railroads, popular sovereignty, or anything else that suited the invaders' purpose. It worked again and again and, as will be seen, could be used to justify deferred or deficient annuity distributions, to rationalize interdenominational bickering as Christian leaders fought for their share of the Indian civilization fund, and to soothe the nerves of white men as they observed Indian women and children in a state of starvation.[11]

While Manypenny returned to Indian country to negotiate treaties that diminished the size of nine reservations but in no way implied that the Indians were to be wholly removed from Kansas in the foreseeable future, the Indian issue in Congress became engulfed in a sea of rhetoric. True, a few legislators took a stand on the side of the tribes, but in retrospect their voices were cries in the wilderness. Responding to the argument that not including the Indian reserves within the actual jurisdiction of the proposed territory was a guarantee of Indian rights, Congressman James Meacham of Vermont suggested that "you might as well say that your heart is not included in your body." "I will not say that [locating eighteen tribes in the proposed territory] was done to prevent that territory denied to slavery from being occupied by free whites," said William Seward of New York, "but it has that effect. Where will they go? Back across the Mississippi? Where will it stop—the Himalayas?" "Methinks I see the Indian urged on by the advancing wave pressing westward, till he finds himself in view of the Pacific ocean," offered Congressman S. H. Walley of Massachusetts, "and as his eyes look in vain for other lands to which he may retire, he feels the force of the waves of the Pacific turned against him and pressing him backward toward the Rocky Mountains." A comparison between blacks and Indians in future Kansas Territory was at the very center of the debate, as E. M. Chamberlain of Indiana was quick to point out in a statement bordering on the prophetic. Insisting that the African slave might be civilized for the reason that he could be enslaved, the less docile Indian enjoyed no such advantage.

"You cannot civilize the Indian," he said, "because you cannot enslave him." Creating a Kansas Territory would be a national disaster, for it would only hasten the Indians' extinction. "Their bones—their very ashes—will be converted into bread to pamper their destroyers," he predicted, "and we may profitably abandon that more precarious enterprise—plundering guano from the South America coast. We have two whole races of men to use up for the same purpose—the bones and ashes of one, and the sweat and tears of the other."[12]

However, by the time the halls of Congress echoed with such pronouncements the emigrant reserves in Kansas were already overrun by squatters and speculators unconcerned with legal niceties, sectional differences, or the future of Indian civilization. Manypenny continued to be the scapegoat. One writer to a Missouri newspaper criticized his spineless diplomacy as the work of an armchair expert "not so well qualified to judge the Indian at home in the wigwam or around the council fire as those who have spent their lives among these people," and dismissed the government's so-called permanent Indian policy as a crumbling barrier to "emigration now beating upon the eastern boundary of this Territory." Senator Stephen A. Douglas of Illinois, presidential hopeful, sponsor of the Kansas-Nebraska Bill, and indefatigable champion of popular sovereignty, insisted the bill would provide adequate protection for the person and property of the Indians, while Representative Taylor of Ohio was persuaded that "fair and honest" treaties were all that the Indians wanted or needed.[13]

Oversimplified generalizations of this sort were politically motivated and, from the Indians' point of view, contrary to fact—as can be seen in the events surrounding the Delaware treaty Manypenny negotiated in 1854. Because it displayed in intricate detail virtually every scheme and trick that could be deployed in the assault on Indian land, the Delaware debacle may be viewed as an introduction and even a guide to tribal destruction and removal from Kansas in general. On the surface this particular treaty seemed not at all controversial, in that it ceded the typical block of trust land to be sold under the supervision of the executive branch, in return for annuities and a more concentrated reservation along the eastern border of Kansas. Apparently, Manypenny was convinced the arrangement would satisfy even the most excessive demands of those who coveted land west of Missouri, particularly since the Kansas-Nebraska Bill (which became law between the date the treaty was negotiated and the date it was proclaimed) specifically provided that Indian rights and property in the new territory were to remain inviolate unless specifically extinguished by additional treaties. In this he was sadly mistaken. But when he perceived the utter contempt the intruders had for *any* Delaware claim to land in Kansas and tried to do something about it, the commissioner was chastised by the squatters as a "damn, hypocritical scamp." Following his replacement by a more cooperative commissioner, General James Denver, Manypenny was described as a "son of a bitch" by George W. Ewing, one of the most powerful land brokers who ever operated west of the Mississippi. Perhaps the worst that should be said of Manypenny is that he was a slow learner, and the best is that against tremendous odds he did his best to alter the direction of Indian affairs in Kansas. He advised Interior secretary Robert McClelland that the rape of the Delaware trust lands "had the most pernicious influence, the effects of which are but too visible in the Territory," and he was in total agreement with Delaware agent Benjamin F. Robinson when the latter inquired of the Indian Office, "Are treaties merely made for fun, and hence to be looked on as maneuvers played off for the benefit of a hungry crowd of land speculators?"[14]

The "hungry crowd" was a combination of town speculators from Missouri and military officers from nearby Fort Leavenworth who planned the Leavenworth town site while the Delaware treaty awaited ratification. To them it made no difference that the treaty invoked the federal statute of March 3, 1807, which authorized the forceful (if necessary) expulsion of intruders on ceded Indian land, or that Manypenny and surveyor John C. McCoy protested their illegal actions. On July 14, three days before the Delaware treaty was proclaimed, the promoters brazenly informed the local land office that they were "laying out a town." They claimed to have inside information regarding the limits of the Delaware survey; they justified their admittedly "permature" activity on grounds that they were being pressured by competing town promoters; and to add insult to injury, they chastised Manypenny for having failed to publicize the treaty "until two and one-half months after it was concluded." Manypenny was understandably furious. Emphasizing that the town-site claim consisted of only "four log cabins and no land broken or fenced," he denounced the scheme as wholly nefarious and the speculators' insistence that they were "innocent squatters with large investments" as absolutely absurd. The Delawares expected the military to come to their rescue, but with at least some of the Fort Leavenworth officialdom heavily involved in the scheme, such relief was out of the question. Still less comforting to the Indians was the federal statute of July 22, 1854, which, in a remarkable capitulation to squatter pressure on the Kansas border, allowed all Indian lands to which title had been or should be extinguished to come under the very liberal provisions of the Preemption Law of 1841. Squatters had up to three months to file claims after the surveys had been completed. But it was not until November 2, 1854, that the first survey contract was let for the Leavenworth town site, and not until January 12 that the first official plats were forwarded to Washington. Manypenny was dismayed and solicited a ruling from a higher authority. It came on August 12, 1854, when the attorney general of the United States ruled that the law of 1807 took precedence. He further held that the Leavenworth promoters were intruders on the public domain, and that the War Department should see to it that they were expelled. However, in a memorandum to President Pierce, acting Interior secretary George C. Whiting cautioned that the expenses would have to be paid out of the Delaware annuities. Furthermore, innocent people might get hurt, and, in any case, the deployment of military force in such instances was "discordant to the feelings of the people of the United States." Clearly, Whiting's reasoning was comforting to the intruders:

> The bold and enterprising have for a long period of years been not only permitted, but encouraged by the general policy of the government with regard to the public lands to press forward in advance of the more natural and steady progress of settlement, and secure as a reward for the hardships and expenses they incurred, more valuable lands for themselves. Indeed, so frequently has Congress enacted laws for the protection of persons who have settled on the public lands, prior to such settlements being authorized by law, that the Act of 1807 has long since been lost sight of or regarded as obsolete.

One month later the executive branch was again requested to expel the Delaware intruders, but by this time such action was a dead letter.[15]

Reflecting on the awesome implications of the Leavenworth speculation, Manypenny observed, "What a spectacle for the view of the statesman, philanthropist, Christian—a subject for the most profound consideration and reflection. With reservations dotting the eastern portion of the Territory, there they stand, the representatives and remnants of tribes once as powerful and dreaded as they are now weak and dispirited." Pro-slave and free-soil fanatics were becoming strange bedfellows, so much so that by 1857 a Washington newspaper was prompted to conclude that slavery in Kansas was secondary to the mania for land and railroad speculation. Treaty-making on the Delaware model was the name of the game, with trust lands, diminished reserves, individual allotments, alienation, and ultimate removal the logical steps to be followed in "civilizing" the Kansas tribes. And the extent to which the Indian leaders were conditioned to the new dispensation can be seen in the words of a frontier editor, who in 1858 reported, "[They] have a knowledge of but two places—Kansas and Washington—and when one has been away from the Territory for any length of time it may be supposed, of course, that he has been to the capitol."[16]

On July 10, 1855, Agent Benjamin Robinson bitterly declared that military ejection of the Leavenworth speculators was "no longer looked for." This was the signal for others to spring into action. Obviously cognizant of what Manypenny called "the lawlessness first introduced into Kansas by the military officers at Fort Leavenworth," Charles Robinson, head of the New England Emigrant Aid Society and the first statehood governor of Kansas, engineered an illicit timber-cutting contract with Delaware chief Sarcoxie, who later repudiated the arrangement, apparently in an effort to save face with his own people. In the summer of 1856 violence erupted on the Shawnee reservation near Westport, ostensibly over the slavery issue, but in fact over timber claims, town sites, and prime squatter land. Shawnee agent William Gay was shot within sight of his agency headquarters. Murderers, desperadoes, and robbers roamed the countryside at will. According to Osage River agent Maxwell McCaslin, the Shawnees were faced with "an absolute reign of terror." McCaslin promptly requested that the intruders be expelled with dispatch and brought to justice; yet his knowledge of the Delaware debacle caused him to temper his natural response and, ultimately, to suggest a more moderate course. Many of the intruders had journeyed thousands of miles to seek homes in Kansas; most were God-fearing heads of respectable families; winter was approaching, food was in short supply, children were sickly, and, since the intruders had "no where else to go," McCaslin was convinced that justice should be deferred until the following spring—which, as it turned out, left the intruders in control of their Shawnee claims indefinitely. Virtually the same pattern of events transpired on the Miami reserve. Indeed, it should be emphasized that these unfortunate developments were no exception to the rule, and that for proof of this one need only examine Secretary McClelland's directive to Manypenny in the fall of 1855 to appreciate the full force of the government's position regarding Indian affairs in Kansas

Territory. President Pierce had decided to *allow* the military to expel intruders on Indian reservations, but they were cautioned "to go very slow." Notices were to be posted in public places, plenty of discussion was to be allowed, careful records of all proceedings were to be kept, and, above all, "a reasonable amount of time" was to pass before the military would be ordered into action. As for the Indian agents who might find themselves in a difficult position, "Prudence and moderation should characterize the conduct of the agents of the department and the exercise thereof should be strongly inculcated in the instructions to them."[17]

Executive indecision and military inaction were profound devices in the removal of Indians from Kansas, but there were other techniques no less significant. Fused to the concept of a freedom-oriented white yeomanry dating back to the days of Jefferson, squatter integrity was a mighty antidote to the alleged evils of speculative monopoly in the assault on tribal land. In almost routine manner it became fashionable to rationalize illegal squatter residence on Indian reservations on grounds that to do otherwise was to invite the more sinister machinations of big business. For example, shortly after the Kansas-Nebraska Bill was passed and the Delaware land opened to intrusion, a spokesman for the Missouri squatters wrote Manypenny that unless a "substitution treaty" were negotiated that would give the squatters more confidence in themselves, the trust lands would fall into the hands of "monopolists." What they feared, of course, was the unwelcome prospect of bidding for their fraudulent claims against interests with greater resources and political influence. They even brought forth the bizarre argument that the Delawares themselves were on their side, and that if the Indian Office did not see it their way the real intent of the government would be compromised. This Manypenny flatly denied, but his efforts were in vain.[18]

The Council Grove town speculation against the Kansa Indians on their Neosho River reserve in east-central Kansas, which began in the preterritorial period and continued well into the statehood period, is one of the more classic examples

of how squatter-monopolist competition and conflicting surveys contributed to the illegal seizure of Indian land. But
there were others. Repeatedly, the literature of Indian Kansas demonstrates the rewards that accrued to squatters and
land jobbers as they took advantage of government preoccu-
pation with the slavery controversy. A not uncommon tactic
was to get the jump on a competitor the moment a cession
treaty was negotiated, complain about pro-slavery aggres-
sion, construct some crude form of improvement, and then,
when the government survey finally established that the claim
was fraudulent, to demand title to the land on preemptory
rights and/or compensation for work accomplished. Indian
agents literally flooded the Indian Office in Washington with
requests for survey charts and more precise information
regarding the seemingly endless relocation of reservation
boundaries. On November 3, 1855, for example, Agent
George Clarke reported that in the absence of legal guide-
lines he was unable to do anything about several hundred
squatters who had invaded the Potawatomi reserve near
Topeka. Agent McCaslin reported similar developments on
the Miami, Peoria, and Kaskaskia reserves. Worse, the Indian Office in Washington had refused to provide him with
any instructions whatsoever regarding alternative courses of
action. This was not surprising since later it was determined
that on behalf of his "southern constituents" who in "good
faith" had taken "great risks" investing in Indian land, a
well-connected politician had exerted tremendous pressure
on the Interior Department to allow the forces of popular
sovereignty to have their way in Kansas. Meanwhile, there
also were conflicting claims involving allotments to tribal
leaders who had been party to nefarious treaty negotiations,
but who on numerous occasions were no less confused than
the white intruders regarding what lands were in fact theirs.
As it became obvious that the Pierce and Buchanan adminis-
trations were pursuing a policy of calculated vacillation on
Indian policy, intrusions on Indian land took on an air of
respectability and finally were used as justification for additional treaties that would accomplish the wholesale expul-

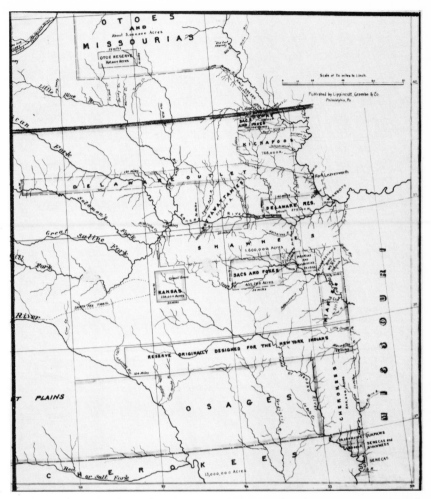

A portion of Captain Seth Eastman's Map of Nebraska and Kansas Territories, 1854, indicating the locations of the various Indian reserves in eastern Kansas during the early territorial years. *Courtesy Cartographic Branch, National Archives.*

OTTAWA

FIRST BOOK.

CONTAINING

LESSONS FOR THE LEARNER;

PORTIONS OF

THE GOSPEL BY LUKE,

OMITTED BY

MATTHEW AND JOHN;

AND

THE OTTAWA LAWS.

BY

JOTHAM MEEKER,

MISSIONARY OF

THE AMER. BAP. MIS. UNION.

Second Edition.

Ottawa Baptist Mission Station.

J. MEEKER, PRINTER,

1850.

OTAWA

MUSENAIKUN.

EUE KO

WLKI UKENOUMATEWIN;

KUER ANINT

OMLN·WAHIMOWIN NOK,

KAPWA OLEPEUMOWAT

MRTO KUER HAN;

KUER OTAWAK

OTEEPAKONIKEWINIWAN.

UWI TUL

WRLTOT UHIHAK,

RNONIKOHIN

KEHIMOKOMANEWE FRPTISUN.

Nalif Wrlhikatrk.

Otawa Prptise Kuteiturwtikumitof.

UHIHAK, MRSENAIKUNIKRT,

1850.

The title page of a book containing a portion of the Gospel by Luke and the Ottawa Laws translated from English into the Ottawa language and printed by the Reverend Jotham Meeker. *Courtesy Kansas State Historical Society.*

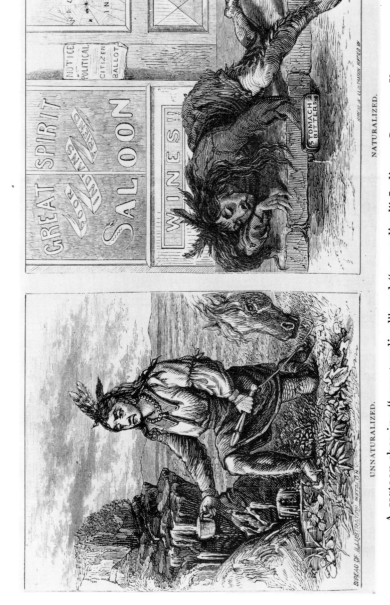

A cartoon showing "unnaturalized" and "naturalized" Indians. *Courtesy Kansas State Historical Society.*

A traditional Sac and Fox bark house. *Courtesy Kansas State Historical Society.*

An engraving, made in 1906, of Captain Joseph Parks' rather elegant home in Johnson County. *Courtesy Kansas State Historical Society.*

A drawing by George Catlin of the Sac and Fox begging dance. *Courtesy Kansas State Historical Society.*

Prairie Band Potawatomis dressed to perform a dance in Topeka, 1925. *Courtesy Kansas State Historical Society.*

Moses Keokuk, Sac and Fox, shortly before his death in 1903.
Courtesy Kansas State Historical Society.

Louis View, Potawatomi chief. *Courtesy Kansas State Historical Society.*

sion of the tribes. Writing to President Lincoln in 1862, Caleb B. Smith, secretary of the Interior, bluntly demanded that another Shawnee treaty was needed to "clear the confusion" resulting from the erroneous reservation boundaries established in 1854.[19]

A particularly effective device utilized by the intruders was the private claim association. Although these associations were theoretically designed to checkmate the more affluent and politically sophisticated jobbers, a more practical consideration was to neutralize the federal courts in Kansas Territory. The resolves of the Miami Claim Association provide an excellent illustration:

> Resolved, that as law abiding citizens we deem it a duty to call together our neighbors to know whether we shall be ruined by vexatious and unjust law suits brought in our Federal Courts under pretended sympathy for the Miami Indians. Resolved, that under existing circumstances it is our duty to take immediate and prompt steps for our protection and to prevent the ruinous consequences that will accrue to this portion of *our* [italics added] Territory if the action of the present Grand Jury is sustained. Resolved, that as good citizens we wish to abide by the laws of our country and our God—but we believe that the action of the Grand Jury, if maintained, will deprive us of our liberty, our peace, our prosperity, and will be ruinous to our country at large.

These same law-abiding citizens, it should be emphasized, were also engaged in the whiskey traffic among the Miamis. In 1847 Congress had attempted to strengthen the whiskey prohibition clauses of the 1834 Trade and Intercourse Act by certifying Indians as competent witnesses against those who distributed the illicit commodity. Yet, because the profits were so immense and federal officials so hopelessly involved in the removal of the tribes, the law was widely disregarded. Some of the techniques to disguise the circumvention of justice bordered on the bizarre, as can be seen in an 1853 report of Sac and Fox agent B. A. James. In that year Kis-ke-to-no, an inconsequential Sac and Fox leader, was incarcerated in a dungeon until he promised that his people would no longer engage in the consumption of whiskey. The Kickapoo agency headquarters in 1860 were located next to a town named Kennekuk, where "whiskey was the entire business," while on the nearby Potawatomi reserve it was reported that a fair distribution of annuities was impossible because of "the free flow of whiskey." But for the truly tragic dimensions of the problem, although it was then couched in a light vein, one need only reflect on the account of a reporter who stopped by the "Quindaro Brewery" in 1858, a place which today is within the limits of metropolitan Kansas City:

> The bright eyes of [a Delaware girl] attracted me in. Bareheaded—her long black hair was somewhat disheveled; but she seemed none the less attractive for that. Her person was not scrupulously clean, but she was a child of nature, and cleanliness belongs to civilization. Observing that I was admiring her, she came up, slapped me on the back, and said in good English, "You treat me?" Who could resist such an appeal? I treated![20]

In view of the seemingly unobstructed manner in which the Indians of territorial Kansas were exploited, the perceptive reader will inquire: How was it that the removal program was so easily inaugurated? Where was the territorial leadership? Why did the leaders not intervene? Were they so naïve as not to know what was going on before their very eyes? The answer is as complex as it is simple—complex in that unusual circumstances prevailed which provided a smokescreen that with a few important exceptions has clouded the issue to this day, and simple in that the territorial leadership was involved in the scheme from the start.

Consider, for example, the words of A. T. Andreas, the most influential nineteenth-century historian of Kansas, on the subject of Andrew H. Reeder, governor of the territory from June 29, 1854, until his forced resignation on July 28, 1858. A native of Easton, Pennsylvania, "a most ardent and loyal Democrat . . . who had never been a politician in the sense of seeking or holding public office, but was, at the time of his appointment, considered one of the most honest, able, well-balanced, clear-headed, reliable, Democratic, Kansas-Nebraska, popular sovereignty lawyers in the country," Reeder was characterized by historian Andreas as the unfortunate victim of the slavocracy—one who never flinched in the face of the enemy and who under all circumstances performed his public duties with honor and integrity. True, he "had become vulnerable to the shafts of his enemies by becoming interested, like many other citizens, in the lots of various embryo cities"—as, for example, in Leavenworth, Lawrence, Tecumseh, Topeka, and Pawnee. True, "he had got them at cheaper rates than possible except in consideration of his official position." But this is not why he was forced to resign. "The scheme was to remove Andrew J. Reeder, the official land-speculator, and thus be rid of an honest governor, whom neither threats could intimidate nor bribes induce to countenance the outrages on law and decency which they [the pro-slave interests] had committed." No mention was made of Indians.[21]

Excepting the rather cryptic reference to land speculation, such analysis was unfair and, in view of the evidence, mostly contrived. Yet the general picture of territorial Kansas remained virtually unaltered until such twentieth-century historians as Hodder, Malin, Nichols, and Gates pointed in a different direction. Even so, the full importance of Reeder's role against the Indians remains to be understood, as does his remarkable influence on those who helped engineer the end of Indian Kansas. As governor of a territory with a high concentration of semi-acculturated Indians faced with unprecedented problems of survival, Reeder was in a position to exemplify either the best or the worst kind of leadership. While he did not hold the official title Ex Officio Superintendent of Indian Affairs, as did a number of other territorial governors, his superiors nevertheless made it abundantly clear that at all times he was to be concerned with the welfare of the Indians and that "he should be the last to set an example at variance with the uniform practices of the Indian Bureau." This he brazenly refused to do. He speculated in half a dozen territorial towns that were located on Indian land; he became financially involved in the strategic and exceedingly valuable tracts near Topeka which belonged to Kansa half-breeds; he convened the first meeting of the territorial legislature at Pawnee, which, had this remote town become the permanent capital of Kansas, would have made for him a fortune in town lots. On occasion he used public funds to finance his real-estate adventures; he encouraged other officials to follow in his footsteps; and when some of these individuals presented him with too much competition he accused them of subversion and plots to overthrow his administration. But most important of all, he did everything in his power to discredit Manypenny's influence on behalf of the Indians.[22]

Whatever else he may have been, Manypenny was no fool, and by the early months of 1855 he was well informed regarding Reeder's machinations. He advised the appropriate authorities in Washington, which precipitated an immediate and inflammatory response from Reeder. Vindictive, irrational, and threatening not only to the Indians but to Manypenny himself, the letter is worth recounting in detail:

> You [Manypenny] say this is demoralizing to the Indians and the whites. You say this [land speculation] discloses a condition of things among the Federal officers which if not soon rebuked must produce a state of demoralization in the Territory, the effects of which will be as lamentable as the acts themselves are disgraceful. You have raised an issue with me which must be settled not in a corner but in the full blaze of day. It is no less grave a question than whether on the one hand we are dishonest, dishonorable men guilty of revolting fraud, or whether you are a vile and unscrupulous slanderer

who does not recognize the binding obligations of truth and justice or the sacredness of private reputation. I assert the latter and I will prove it before I am done with you . . . . If I win you leave office and vice versa. You have sown your miserable, baseless, inexcusable calumny broadcast over the Union; and now I solicit, I challenge, I defy you to this test. If there is a spark of manliness in your composition you will not shrink from it.[23]

Manypenny did not ignore the challenge, particularly after the aging Thomas Hart Benton came to Reeder's rescue. Responding to a letter published in the *National Intelligencer,* in which Benton rebuked Manypenny for having exceeded his authority in certifying vouchers relating to Indian claims and land deals in Kansas Territory, the commissioner retorted:

Now sir, led on by you, I defy them all. If they can strike another blow, let them level it; if they can invent another slander, let them utter it. I dare their worst efforts, and hold their conduct, and yours, sir, in unreserved contempt. . . . I have resisted from all quarters and from all men, the wonderful efforts which have been made to improperly obtain Indian lands and Indian money . . . . I will *not allow* the Indians to be plundered . . . whether attempted by the practiced and professional Indian operator or by official dignitaries or soldiers. . . . We are in strange times. One State [Missouri] proposes to punish any citizen who shall aid in carrying out a certain law of the United States; a Governor, elsewhere [in Kansas], to have a United States officer turned out of office because he interposes the laws and regulations of the Indian Department. . . . [And] an ex-Senator of thirty years' standing invites a suit and publicly rails against an officer because he will not imitate a Bible character, as the Senator puts it, in passing upon accounts, but chooses rather to rewrite receipts and vouchers executed in conformity with law and regulations.[24]

Commissioner Manypenny's strictures led to Reeder's removal, although it was three years before this was accomplished—due in large measure to a vacillating President Pierce, who complained that the Kansas problem "haunted him day and night." In the meantime, the assault on the Indian reserves continued along the course plotted by Reeder. Territorial attorney Andrew J. Isaacs, territorial secretary Daniel Woodson and Kansas associate justices S. W. Johnson and Rush Elmore—to name a few—speculated in trust lands without restraint. When their actions were questioned, they simply and effectively cried foul in the name of popular sovereignty. Ely Moore, federal registrar at the Lecompton land office, openly issued certificates of preemption to intruders on the Miami reserve. These certificates became the object of speculation and, according to the Indian Office, were used to defraud unsuspecting emigrants. A New York Christian chief advised the Indian Office in 1858 that his predecessor's life had been threatened for having refused to agree to a land sale arranged by attorney Isaacs. Reports of squatters resorting to brute force became increasingly commonplace; Indian agents were physically abused and forced to abandon their agencies, and by the time the territorial period came to an end the formula for Indian removal was only too clear.[25]

Kansas became a state on January 29, 1861. In its official seal were inscribed the words, "Ad astra per aspera" ("To the stars through difficulty"). Most Americans viewed the motto within the context of slavery and the impending civil conflict. But for the repeatedly displaced emigrant Indians the phrase had a very different meaning.

CHAPTER TWO

The Capitalization of Nature

ONE OF THE MOST IMPORTANT definable psychological bases for the dissolution of tribal hegemony over the Kansas region was the powerful appeal of white assumptions concerning the proper uses of nature. Since colonial times, it had been argued that God did not intend for His natural bounty to be left unexploited and that therefore Indian control of such a natural storehouse as North America was intended as a temporary stage in the evolutionary scheme of Providence. The idea that the Great Plains was a desert, a premise which was convincing to at least some observers in the first third of the nineteenth century, contributed to its being for a time acceptable as a home for the dislocated tribes of the East. By 1854, however, it was evident that Kansas was anything but a desert in terms of natural resources, and that inevitably the old argument about the intentions of the Deity for the aborigines was no longer tenable.

By mid-century, as the reader of such books as Leo Marx's *The Machine in the Garden* or David Emmons' *Garden in the Grasslands* becomes quickly aware, the concept of the potential capitalization of nature—the conversion of geographic elements, which could otherwise only be passively enjoyed as scenery, into a myriad of usable forms—had become a kind of frenzy with white Americans. They, after all, possessed nothing if not real estate, especially if Indian claims could be extinguished. Baldwin Möllhausen, a German artist traveling with a Pacific railway surveying party in 1853, came to the conclusion that so taken were people with the idea that nature was the handmaiden of pecuniary accumulation that they could no longer perceive nature in its virgin state. Seeing a forest, he wrote, Americans envisaged houses, mills, and factories, and were seriously diverted from their enjoyment of a long prairie view by mental calculations of board feet and bushels per acre. Legal scholars Robert McCloskey and James Willard Hurst have also suggested, and this study would support their argument, that the American concept of the purpose and uses of its constitution and laws was radically altered in the nineteenth century so that it might better comport with the economic drives of the nation, to which resource exploitation was basic.[1]

The history of the capitalization of nature as related to the Indian reserves in Kansas is, therefore, an excellent introduction to the American character in this period, as well as a guide to some of the deep-seated elements of cross-cultural interaction. There was an evangelical attempt, often successful, to convince portions of the tribes that the excitement of changing the form of nature to fit man's will and to enlarge his material comfort was as irresistible to the Indian as to the white. Railroad promoters initially argued that a simple path was needed to connect the states, but they soon perceived that Indian lands were obtainable by clever lobbyists, that tribal funds might be directed into railroad securities, and that subsidiary timber operations might fuel the corporation's financial as well as iron engines. The organization and institutionalization of Kansas natural resources led to the creation of a transportation network, and to the various natural resource industries, such as timber milling and coal mining, which the railroad spawned. In addition, the railroad connected Indian Kansas with markets, the *sine qua non* of commercial exploitation of tribal lands. These events were basic in that they first gave these Indian lands "value" in the sense that, once grasped, they seemed to excite all those involved, regardless of their cultural affiliation, causing them to vie for control of the speculative process. When that process and the assumptions behind it were tentatively accepted by the government and the tribes, the situation ultimately became inconsistent with the possibility of leaving the timbered and fertile soil of the region in control of Indian tribes who utilized its raw material only slightly. It is important, therefore, to analyze when, where, and why the capitalization of nature as it impinged on Indian lands in Kansas began, and how it developed *vis-à-vis* tribal perceptions of their interests and the government's estimate of its legal obligations.

The groundwork for the exploitation of natural resources in Kansas was established in the treaties of the 1850s and 1860s. The Delaware treaty of 1854 stated that since the inevitable settlement of lands ceded by Kansas tribes would require the creation of transportation facilities, the Delawares must allow rights of way through lands retained by them on the same terms as was common for the location of similar facilities through the lands of United States citizens. Of course the tribe was not granted any of the rights of United States citizens. Railroad companies had only to pay just compensation for damages to be assured of blanket permission to penetrate the Delaware lands whenever they thought it necessary. The 1854 treaties with the Shawnees, the Sacs and Foxes, the confederated Kaskaskias, and the Miamis, as well as the 1859 treaty with the Kansas and the 1865 Osage treaty, contained the same wording regarding transportation development. One might ask why these tribes did not demand that some limit be placed upon access to their reserves by outside corporations, as for example the Cherokees did in their treaty of 1866. The answer is that by 1866 the negative impact of railroad intrusion upon tribal sovereignty was apparent from the Kansas example. Treaties negotiated in the 1850s with tribes to the south of Kansas, such as the treaty with the Choctaws in 1855, are similar to the Kansas negotiations. Also, Cherokee caution was due partly to the desire of that tribe to organize its own railroads rather than to a tribal consensus on their undesirability. There was really no reason for the Indians to suspect in 1854, or for nearly ten years thereafter, that industrialization of tribal lands would necessarily result in the removal or destruction of their national cohesion. Only when the railroads began to build in earnest during and after the Civil War did the hidden designs implicit in but not necessarily following from the wording or omissions in the treaties become clear. The future would be determined by thousands of individual day-to-day decisions on matters not formally regulated by such broad statements of intent as treaties or laws. It might well be argued that the Indian mistake in signing treaties with right-of-way clauses resulted not from their misunderstanding of the documents themselves or from coercion but from a miscalculation of what whites could and would make of them. The same set of treaties might well have heralded the beginning of a very different sort of story, although in retrospect this seems highly improbable.[2]

In fact, treaties in the early sixties went much further in the use of Indian lands to promote railroads. The Delaware treaty of 1860 included a tribal belief that a railroad through their reservation would enhance the value of lands in the area allotted to individual Indians. They therefore gave the Leavenworth, Pawnee & Western railroad an option to purchase lands ceded by the tribe and not allotted to Indians, provided that the company should build a line and begin disposing of the land to white settlers within seven years. The next year, when the first payment came due, the railroad had not yet succeeded in converting the land option into ready cash support from the East. Responding to this, Thomas Ewing, Jr., a railroad company agent who had learned the business of converting a debit to a credit while in business as an Indian trader in Indiana, had a conference with the new president, Abraham Lincoln, resulting in the supplemental treaty of 1861. This allowed the company to pay the tribe in bonds rather than cash—bonds secured by the promise of the land. The Potawatomi treaty of 1861 involved that tribe as well within the designs of the L.P. & W. by giving the company the option to purchase lands of that tribe at a minimum price of $1.25 an acre. The Kickapoo treaty of 1862 created a similar situation to the benefit of the Atchison & Pike's Peak railroad, with Samuel Pomeroy, Kansas senator, president. In 1866 the Delawares agreed to remove to the south and sell the last substantial body of their lands to the Missouri River railroad company.[3]

There are three possible interpretations of these treaties: the Indians were coerced into signing them and their protest was largely throttled; they were too foolish or culturally isolated to have any opinion; or there appeared to be some real advantages to the tribes in the legal proceedings. The third of these is the most reasonable. In his recent account of New England Indians in the seventeenth century Alden Vaughn has convincingly demonstrated that tribes of small population residing on large bodies of land were not always unwilling to sell parts of their domain. None of the initial set of Kansas treaties ceding land to railroads provided for sale of all the lands of any tribe nor its removal; it was only provided that there would be a sharing of the land by both cultures to the presumed benefit of both. Once the decision to cede some land was made, there were excellent reasons for the tribe to sell directly to a railroad rather than to transfer valuable tracts in trust to the United States or to individuals by sealed bid or at auction. The land could be sold in a block, the worst along with the best. Sealed-bid auctions, while they yielded some very high prices on certain parcels, often did not result in an average price of more than $1.25, with some land remaining unsold. Also, the cost of surveying the land, appraising it, and transferring title to individuals would be paid by the railroad rather than the tribe, as in the case of sealed-bid sales or auctions. Third, the money would presumably come to the tribe immediately, or at least relatively quickly as compared with the option of transferring title to the government in trust. Some tribes contracted with attorneys at high percentages to collect money owed them by the government for sales of property going back thirty years or earlier. For example, the Choctaws were still fighting in the 1880s to collect money from their lands in the Southeast ceded in trust to the government in the 1830s. Last, and certainly not least, if nature were to be capitalized, might not the Indian share in the spoils through an increase in the value of lands still held by either the tribe or individual Indians?

Assuming their proper enforcement, a careful examination of these treaties reveals some substantial provisions for the protection of Indian rights. Each begins with a preface stating the belief that "it will contribute to the civilization of their people to dispose of a portion of their present reservation in Kansas" and then goes on to explain that railroad development will enhance the value of tribal land. That the sale options had definite conditions, which for years was the case regarding federal land grants to transcontinental roads, is likely to escape the attention of scholars determined to prove that treaties were a sham from the start. For one thing, there were construction time requirements as there were in the land grant bills. The railroad could not get title to the land until the road was built. Generally, title came in two parts, the first half when the road was half completed through the reserve, and the rest upon completion. The Potawatomi treaty of 1861 required the railroad to build halfway through in six years and the rest of the way in the next three. The Kickapoo treaty of 1862 required that fifteen miles be built in three years and the rest in the next three, with no title to be passed until the project was completed. The Delaware treaty of 1860 was similar. Also, once the patent was obtained, the roads were not allowed to hold the lands for speculation. The Delaware treaty allowed the road seven years after getting the patents to sell the land, and any land not sold by that time would revert to the tribe for sale by sealed bids. The Kickapoo and Potawatomi treaties allowed five years for the railroad to settle the country. Payment was provided for in various ways, but, in any case, all treaties specified that any default by the railroad in interest or principal or any change in construction schedules would result in its forfeit of the land. The roads were allowed to take necessary materials for construction upon paying damages, *except timber.* Since during the construction phase the Indians would still hold title to the land, the roads were required to pay the tribes a royalty for all timber used. Significantly, this last proviso was widely abused in practice. The point, however, is that the treaties were not responsible for this abuse. In fact, the government was given some formidable weapons to protect its interests. It could call for forfeit by the roads for noncompliance, and it could punish the road for depredations which it refused to pay for by compensating the Indians from a trust fund of bonds which treaties required the road to deposit. In the case of the Kickapoos this was an amount double the value of the lands.[4]

True, the treaty process was often corrupted so that the true will of the majority was unclear, as will be seen in the case of the Kickapoo treaty of 1862. True, tribal law allowed citizenship to those marrying Indians regardless of their racial "Indianness," thus blurring the distinction between the tribe as a political entity and a traditional culture. Yet evidence is strong that, as in other techniques used with Indians in Kansas, the carrot-and-stick technique was more common than the club. The Choctaws and Cherokees just south of Kansas went so far as to subscribe stock as tribes in potential railroads even before any treaty was negotiated requiring them to grant rights of way. The Delaware trust fund, which was established from the sale of the Delaware lands, was invested, with their consent, in securities of the Union Pacific, Eastern Division railroad, successor to the L.P. & W. Trust funds of other Kansas tribes were invested by the federal government in state or railway stock, with the result that the Indians made massive financial contributions to the very corporations that were contributing to their destruction. In one of the most controversial cases regarding the transfer of Indian lands to a railway, the Osages in 1865 and again in 1868 expressed a clear desire that their lands be sold to the Leavenworth, Lawrence & Galveston and the

Union Pacific, Southern Branch (M.K. & T.) railroads in order that they might obtain ready cash to care for starving Indians who were not particularly interested in pretending to be yeoman farmers. It may be said that without firm evidence of Indian enthusiasm for and participation in the various schemes which, by methods at first unseen, led to tribal dissolution, public opinion in the United States was not so callous as to have supported them without objection. After all, the initial phase was critical because the economic structures involved were then weak and the momentum reversible in a way that was later impossible. James Stone, a principal in the L.P. & W. railroad, confessed to a congressional committee in 1887 that even with options on both the Delaware and Potawatomi reserves, his company was unable, in the early sixties, to attract investment, since "the country was so new to enterprise." A push was required, and it came partly from the Indians, with tragic results few of them intended or foresaw.[5]

Once the treaties were signed and railroad men, land speculators, and timber operators were firmly entrenched on Indian land, the pattern of tribal destruction was something which is wholly apparent, though it requires the full case studies which follow to document it. Indian policy, as reflected in laws and treaties as well as in the hopes of men of good will of both cultures, was distorted cumulatively, a little at a time, by men in the field—businessmen, government officials, and Indians—who were willing to go beyond legal and traditional limits in order that they might pursue individual gain. This process was largely hidden from those outside the limited circle concerned with the routine day-to-day administration, and those who were able to perceive its progress were the same persons who were benefiting directly from the distortions or, all too often and sadly, who were vulnerable to bribery and threats, and so were silent. But this situation eventually deteriorated, and some serious investigations were made which often exposed glaring corruption. From these records the historian can surmise what was going on in the quiet interim between treaties and attempts at reform. Inevitably, however, the time lapse prevented the salvaging of Indian sovereignty in Kansas. The economic momentum developed quickly, and the corporations, once entrenched, involved so many innocent parties that to return to the starting point posed as serious a threat to the economic and political stability of the United States as letting Indian sovereignty continue in the hands of the tribes. At the time of the first treaties, it was quite possible that the Indians and the whites might have coexisted and cross-fertilized each other economically, one giving natural resources and the other technical know-how in a fair exchange. However, when the success of the corporations was allowed, through inadequate control of day-to-day matters, the tragic result was inevitable.

The classic railroad-timber operation, in which both the initial hopeful understandings and their subsequent corruption by men overpowered by lust for money can be clearly seen, was mounted on the Delaware lands in the northeast portion of Kansas. The 1854 treaty provided for sale of lands by sealed bids, and, as explained earlier, excluded preemption by settlers. Surely the 1860 treaty selling to the railroad was a response to the tribe's dissatisfaction with monetary returns from the 1854 settlement. The 1861 supplemental treaty establishing the land mortage and payment in railroad bonds is more controversial. One historian has described this move as a swindle. However, the explanation given by the Delaware agent, Thomas Sykes, who was present at the negotiations, was that the Delawares had originally planned to sell the new land cession by sealed bids as before but became genuinely convinced that sale to a railroad would yield as much money, and at the same time would raise by a greater margin the value of the 100,000 acres the Indians retained. The major complaint about the 1860 treaty came not from the tribe but from a competing railroad, the Kansas Central. M. Howard Irwin, president of that corporation, wrote that Delaware lands might sell for as much as $15.00 an acre, while the L.P. & W. was offering only $1.25. The Delawares were presumably aware of prices lands would bring, since they had already sold a substantial block for an *average* price of not much more than $1.25, minus the costs of the sale. (Some individual choice tracts did bring $15.00.) Irwin also charged that there was no public notice of amendments to the treaty's first draft, which included no reference to railroads. He pointed out that it was "publicly charged that corrupt means [had] been used by certain parties to secure the consent and cooperation of leading Delawares, without which these amendments would not have been ratified by the Nation." That may be, but if bribes were being made, someone had to be cooperating on the other end. The leaders spoke for the railroad sale and the tribe ratified it, which would seem inconceivable to patriots fearful that their very national existence was at stake. As to the 1861 mortgage provision, President Lincoln did not simply send his draft to the Senate. He was quite worried that this scheme might not be acceptable to the tribe and insisted, over some bureaucratic objections, that the supplementary agreement of 1861 be sent separately to the tribe for ratification. It was, and Lincoln was satisfied that tribal acceptance was genuine.[6]

Be that as it may, it seems obvious that the Delawares did not recognize what distortion might be introduced in the practical application of these treaty provisions. It is here that charges of unwarranted presumption upon their desires become supportable—here, behind the cover of Indian "consent," that real fraud begins. For example, the Delaware decision to sell to the railroad is explainable in the light of a report by their agent that whites in the area between 1854 and 1861 had stolen $48,750 worth of timber and $32,227 in other property from the tribe. The Indian Office had been able to get only two convictions of the thieves and no monetary settlement at all. "The condition of the courts and the execution of law in Kansas for the past six years is so notorious," wrote Sykes, "that it is useless for me to comment on it." The documents supporting this sort of discrepancy between stated public policy and bureaucratic execution— the kind which might lead Indians to sell natural resources to a railroad rather than see them stolen and to misjudge the practical effect of treaties—were seen only by government clerks specializing in Indian affairs. They came to the public eye, ironically, only on occasions when competing speculators tattled on each other in the morning papers. This was as true of frauds perpetrated by the railroad corporation as it was of irregularities resulting from treaties prior to that of 1860.[7]

Certainly, a major element in distortion of treaty intent was the complexity introduced because of the multiplicity of interrelated economic interests pursued in the Indian country by the personnel of the L.P. & W. While a full discussion of what was known as the "Indian ring" will be presented in a subsequent chapter, it can be noted here that the railroad could not safely be viewed in isolation with any hope of understanding the motivations of the men involved with it, nor could acquaintance with the affairs of a single tribe reveal the full stakes of their game. George W. Ewing was an Indian trader who held large debts against the tribes, which could be used as leverage for concessions to the railroad company. A. J. Isaacs was a territorial official and speculator in the lands of virtually all Kansas tribes. R. W. Thompson was Ewing's trading partner. Robert Stevens was a trader and had house-building contracts on tribal lands which depended for success upon the timber policy of railroads; as well, he was interested financially in surveying contracts granted each time a cession was made. These men also served on the boards of other railroads seeking Indian rights, directed the fortunes of sawmill operations and town companies on or adjoining Indian lands, and officially or unofficially were able to muster considerable influence both in the courts and the offices of Kansas and Washington politicos. To say there were conflicts of interest is merely to scratch the surface. They used the multiplicity of their interlocking interest to conceal their precise gain or loss and to befuddle Indians and government clerks. They could wield enough influence to stop a presidential commission from investigating charges of fraud in a surveying contract, as they did in 1861. They were able to control the public pronouncements of Senators James Lane and Samuel Pomeroy. Most important, they brazenly began selling Delaware lands immediately after the 1860 treaty was negotiated, long before any construction began or title transferred, taking down payments of any amount through agents located in the mushrooming Kansas towns. They sold timber—firewood, fence rails, and sawed wood—all at a small price, like men out to pocket the maximum before their first payment was due and to move on to more profitable fields if the fragile structure of their speculation collapsed. One observer at the time asked the obvious. Would these speculators, had they been interested primarily or singly in providing the railroad the Indians expected, have promoted the destruction of valuable timber and other resources? Was the promise of a railroad not a diversion used by men whose interest in the maximum exploitation of Indian lands and funds intertribally was far more powerful than any scruples about providing the citizens of Leavenworth or the Delaware tribe with a working railroad?[8]

By 1863, the L.P. & W. had involved itself in nearly every possible kind of activity on the Delaware lands except railroad building. Only five miles of track were built by this time, leading from nowhere to nowhere in a setting where rails could be simply laid on the ground with no preliminary labor. Yet the company was fighting the very settlers it had encouraged to come to Kansas, over the nature of the title it was transferring. Unsure of ultimate land title, disgruntled settlers stopped a railroad land sale in 1862 by force and threatened any who purchased additional land from the company with immediate expulsion. General James Blunt did not wait for them to act but issued an order to the effect that all settlers on the Delaware lands were to be removed by the military until the title situation was better resolved. After all, there was a Civil War in progress. The company used this respite to pressure the Indian Office to have money from Delaware land sales (including eventual revenues from its own bonds pledged to the Delawares) applied to the building of houses for the Indians by R. S. Stevens. It also argued that it owned the islands in the Missouri River and was entitled to take timber to feed the large sawmill operated by the railroad's subsidiary, the Delaware Lumber Company.[9]

The Indians continued to express a desire to help the railroad but became increasingly worried that the benefits to them might be either delayed or nonexistent. There was chronic wrangling about the value of Delaware improvements—barns, fences, crops, and sheds of the Indians which railroad building might damage if it ever got under way. Railroad employees were responsible, according to the Indian agent, for taking wagons belonging to tribal citizens, and breaking them to pieces without paying for them, and for grazing their animals indiscriminately over Indian farms with no offer of compensation. The only thing constructive the company was known to have done during this period was to rename itself, in 1863, the Union Pacific, Eastern Division. "We would like to accommodate the Rail Road Company," wrote tribal officials John Conner and Charles Journeycake in 1862. "We want to help them all we can and will do provided we can and do justice to our people." But what had once seemed reasonable was no longer certain. The Delawares owed money to traders, including George W. Ewing, and were afraid that if they did not soon reap some income from the railway they would be forced to cede more land in order to pay their obligations. The delays, therefore, began to threaten the tribe in a way the original franchise had not. It was difficult to get action from the understaffed Indian Office on these items, or, for that matter, from Congress, which seemed to regard the ratified treaty as the end of its responsibility. And to pressure the company directly was difficult for the Indians since its attention was turned to other creditors who, unlike the Indians, could sue in the federal courts.[10]

By the end of the Civil War it was uncertain whether the U.P.E.D. was financially able to maintain its claim to Delaware lands, and the railroad organization itself was a shambles, with two competing boards of directors. As a desperation move the Delaware Lumber Company was assigned several tracts of land, ostensibly reserved for depots, and began selling lumber. This the secretary of the Interior called a "highhanded outrage," presumably because it made an embarrassing situation public. Senators Pomeroy and Lane came to the rescue, maintaining that "the characters of these gentlemen forbid that they should be engaged in the business of stealing or defrauding the Indians of their timber." This did not prevent the publicizing of information linking the railroad promoters with the purchase of large numbers of "floats" (claims to land to be located later) from tribal leaders who at the treaty table had been paid for their services. It was said that when some Indians objected to the price they had been promised they were removed from the country with no compensation at all. The central superintendent, Thomas Murphy, reported in 1865 that the timber company was taking wood from individual Indian allotments as well as from the lands to which the railroad had only the most shadowy claim. In all, 6,000 ties had been cut and none paid for. Murphy could not get the company to promise to pay for them, even for a mere 2,100. The new Delaware agent, John Pratt, reported no protests from the Indians because, instead of paying royalty money for the timber to the tribe, the company had been passing hush money to Indian leaders who promised to keep the rank-and-file indignation at a level consistent with the rewards of these illicit benefits. Sad to say, even as the sinister nature of such developments came into focus, it fell to the government to take the initiative in suggesting reform, while Indian tribes and railway corporations were yet locked in a contest with the prize unassigned.[11]

Special agent H. Bartling was sent from Washington in 1866 to make an investigation of the Delaware problem. He found ten sawmills working at full speed. The Delawares were not being paid for the timber cut, but it was not being used for railroad purposes and, worse, not even kept in the state. Senator James Lane was found to be a partner in the lumber company, along with J. D. Perry, then president of the U.P.E.D. The railroad company denied legal liability for the affairs of the lumber company, although Bartling was on solid ground when he concluded that there were interlocking directorates. The special agent tried to clarify the matter by visiting individual tribesmen and submitting their claims for timber-taking to a judge presiding over bankruptcy proceedings for the Delaware Lumber Company. The lumber concern, however, had been so depleted of its profits by the railroad that the judge could honestly report that there was no money in its coffers to pay and no *legal* means to hold the railroad company responsible. A pattern was thus set which was central to the destruction of the tribes.[12]

What Bartling and the Indians perceived at this juncture was that legal procedure did not always correspond with justice, nor were laws any guarantee of virtue in men. Tribal traditions, which equated words with actions and promises with deeds, may well have blinded the Indian to the truth that in America unethical action could be sheltered in corporations legally immune from responsibility. The American public meanwhile helplessly accepted the justification that nothing illegal had been done, half believing that Providence must somehow grant to lawmakers wisdom and humanity above that of other men. Incredibly, they continued to believe it even after Justice Holmes argued in *The Common Law* (1881) that law only reflected the standards of a majority, not the will of God or even more sensitive consciences. What was done to the Indians in Kansas was done in the name of the law. The most frightening aspects of the story are not what was done illegally but what was done legally. In 1856 future Kansas senator Samuel Pomeroy stated that Indian lands and railroads were all the rage, and that as long as the system could be made to fit that spirit "we don't think or care now whether the laws are 'bogus' or not." In the face of this and of a statement by the secretary of the Interior that the government had not "the power or inclination" to check the spirit of enterprise on behalf of the Indian, the actions of men like Bartling, while courageous, were largely symbolic. Certainly, any meaningful change at that point was out of the question.[13]

The Delaware treaty of 1866 marked that point in the pattern when corporate momentum in capitalizing nature became, as a practical matter, irreversible. The U.P.E.D. had become a company too well enmeshed in the councils of the mightly to be allowed to fail. Its officials included names of national note like John Frémont and John Palmer Usher. Usher had started out representing the Delaware Indians against the railroad, arguing in 1861 that the failure of the old L.P. & W. to pay for land was a "gross hearted and nefarious fraud." He lost that case and, since he was working on a percentage basis, found himself financially embarrassed. So, letting bygones be bygones, he hired on with the railroad to help lobby for the Potawatomi lands, and did much better. With the Potawatomi treaty safely ratified he became assistant secretary of the Interior in Mr. Lincoln's administration and two years later rose to full cabinet status, never missing an opportunity all the while to help his old friends fighting barbarism in Kansas. Thomas Ewing, Jr., who had the support of Senator James Lane, missed being appointed assistant secretary under Usher. It was later reported that for his help in getting the 1862 Pacific Railroad Bill through Congress Usher received 10,000 shares of Union Pacific stock worth $500,000; R. S. Stevens received 330 shares, Lane 9,400 shares, and Fielding Johnson (Delaware agent) 100 shares. Acres of Delaware and Potawatomi lands were also judiciously distributed by the U.P.E.D.—to members of Congress; to officials in the Indian Office; to Johnson's successor, John Pratt; to religious organizations with interests in tribal welfare; and, as Paul Gates' search of county deeds revealed, to Delaware chiefs as well. Usher's biographer, generally favorable to him, nevertheless admitted that the secretary's bias toward the U.P.E.D. in Kansas "somewhat slanted his administration of the details of Indian affairs" for which he had overall responsibility. At any rate, the U.P.E.D. in 1866 was not an organization to be tampered with. It was a very different group from the one that in 1860 could get the attention of no one east of Leavenworth.[14]

In the treaty of 1866 the government took the remarkable step of agreeing to pay the Delawares on behalf of the U.P.E.D. for land claimed by that corporation. Certainly, this step must be regarded as an unusual public subsidy for a company that had only recently arrived at most favored status. Understandably, the Delaware leadership in that treaty took the equally remarkable and inverse step of agreeing to sell the remainder of their lands and remove the tribe into Indian Territory to the south. The last of their lands went to the Missouri River railroad with which the Delawares had negotiated an informal agreement in 1864, while trying to acquire some much needed cash. The new railroad promised to pay $2.50 an acre for the land in the relatively near future. The chief promoter of this operation was U.P.E.D. investor Thomas Ewing, Jr.[15]

The entry of the Missouri River railroad into the economic scramble created additional difficulties in the administration of Indian policy. It, unlike railroad companies in previous treaty deals, had been required to make immediate payment for the land in specie and to take immediate title. The treaty makers had learned that much. The Delaware Lumber Company recognized no boundaries in its cutting operation and so was rapidly felling timber upon lands now reserved for the Missouri River railroad. The new corporation was fearful that its lands might be stripped of timber before it could get under way, and even more distressed at the attitude of the Delaware establishment which claimed that until the tribe removed it had a right to sell its timber to whom it pleased. Given the fact that the tribe was relinquishing all claim to land in Kansas, except individual allotments, and had nothing further to gain other than a share of the cash to be derived from using its resources, this attitude is understandable. Certainly, the old policy of complaining about indiscriminate cutting ended with the 1866 treaty, as did the possibility of economic coexistence in Kansas. A federal attorney ruled in October, 1866, that the Missouri River railroad owned the timber on the so-called diminished reserve, and that the Indians could not sell it. Murphy also held that the Delaware Lumber Company and

U.P.E.D. actions were unauthorized, but Murphy was in turn charged with being in the pay of the Missouri River company. Meanwhile, Usher created a legal argument in favor of the U.P.E.D. In his view the Missouri River road had only a contingent purchase contract and therefore could not interfere with the actions of a trunk line which was meeting the critical military and postal needs of the country. This was a remarkable switch for the U.P.E.D. regarding the force of contingent contracts since it had actually sold land to which it had only an option to buy. Also the Missouri River railroad was required to, and did, pay immediately for the land. It may well have been Usher's political influence which guaranteed that the government would look the other way, at least for a time, while the U.P.E.D. took timber on the diminished reserve.[16]

In Washington the Indian Office temporized. For one thing, Indian intent was no longer clear. It seemed that the Delaware tribe had expressed by treaty a "clear desire" that the diminished reserve be sold intact to the Missouri River road, and yet they were now insisting that they had the exclusive right to sell to the U.P.E.D. Furthermore, Murphy was greatly worried about pressure from settlers illegally intruding upon the Delaware lands. The courts in Kansas refused to deal with the issue, while the possibility of a military solution was, in view of the Leavenworth town-site speculation, out of the question. Perhaps it might even be viewed as a purely sectional matter, with all its volatile political ramifications. Murphy saw the railroad grants as a way out of this dilemma and had the Delaware agent post notices stating that railroad companies would adopt such measures as they wished to protect their rights. Clearly, the Indian was on the way out, and the government was washing its hands of the affair, thus leaving the fate of its white citizens and red wards to the workings of natural laws and free enterprise. Bartling, who had been assigned to collect royalties from the U.P.E.D. for the Indians, was wholly confused regarding Murphy's pronouncement and the 1866 treaty. "I am in the dark," he wrote Murphy. Yet, he continued, the pressure to allow the U.P.E.D. to cut timber was too great for him to contend with alone, especially since the Delawares, on the claimed authority of Agent Pratt, were issuing cutting permits. Later, when it was apparent that the U.P.E.D. owed the Delawares over $28,000 for unpaid timber royalties, and Murphy was chastised for being in league with the railroad in defrauding them, the beleaguered superintendent obtained a temporary court injunction against further cutting by the U.P.E.D. This was contrary to the order of the Interior secretary, Orville Browning, of October, 1866, to the effect that the Indian Office should not become involved in the fight among railroads for Indian timber. It was also too late to make much difference for the Delawares, since much of their timber was already cut and the tribe was attempting to revitalize itself in the Indian Territory. They were interested in Kansas only because some of their ancestors were buried there, and because money was owed them by those corporations their natural wealth had spawned.[17]

Though the Delaware experience sets the theme for the capitalization of nature, there were interesting variations elsewhere. The U.P.E.D. tried the same thing on the Potawatomi reserve west of Topeka. The 1861 option to the railroad was obtained partly through support of the Catholic Mission there, since the church was promised land and financial support in return for aiding the railroad. The traders were cut in on the deal, and land and stock were distributed in Washington, as was true of the Delaware scheme. Here, however, the railroad never acted upon its option to buy the land, for reasons that reveal, when compared to the Delaware model, just how important might be differences in discretionary judgment on the part of the field officials and Indians in the early posttreaty stages.[18]

First, the Indians in this instance could not be dissuaded from selecting as their individual allotments the prime timbered land on their reserve. U.P.E.D. president John Perry tried to convince the Indian Office that it should interfere with these choices since that land was too exposed to the claims of the white squatters, who might resort to violence against their red neighbors. He was unsuccessful in this, as he was apparently unsuccessful in convincing the Potawatomi agent that any special advice should be given the Indians in the selection of individual lands. The railroad also complained that a good many names were added to the tribal rolls after the 1861 treaty, thus reducing the surplus land available to the railroad after those Indians who wished to take land in severalty as provided in the treaty had made their selections. The process by which citizenship in the tribe was determined and recognized was one of those bureaucratic devices which could have great significance. With the Potawatomis the federal government took a position slightly different from that in the Delaware situation. Federal clerks stated in the Potawatomi case that only the Indians and the government were parties to the treaty, and that the railroad clause was inserted for the benefit of the Indians, not the corporation. Therefore the Indian interest would be considered first "without regard to verbal quibbles." Usher complained that the government was now showing a decided prejudice against the railroad, particularly by allowing the addition to the allotment rolls of Indian children born since the 1861 treaty, and those claiming to be Potawatomis who were arriving in Kansas from distant places. He wrote in 1866:

> I respectfully submit that it is not the best policy to apportion all the best lands of the reserve to Indians. If it is done the result will be that the residue of the lands will be tardily settled by an unthrifty population of bad examples to the Indians, depredating constantly upon them for wood, etc. Violence will ensue and the Indians will be driven off. More than that the company have the right to have such a division of the land as will enable them to settle it. The object of the treaty was to bring this thirty miles square within the influence of civilization.

Nowhere in the treaty was there any such wording. What was happening was a battle of the interpreters, and in this case the railroad interpretation was so unsuccessful in convincing the necessary officials and Indians at the site that in 1868 it decided not to purchase the Potawatomi lands, for the reason that it was not profitable to do so. In addition to the other problems, there was no provision in the Potawatomi treaty for payment in bonds. The company would have been forced to pay in gold or silver within nine years.[19]

These lands were later purchased at a lower price ($1.00 an acre) by the Atchison, Topeka & Santa Fe, whose rails did not even run through them. The basic point is that the capitalization of nature in Kansas did not inevitably produce identical results. Changes in the attitude of those responsible for the execution of laws and treaties, subtle switches in their assumptions or perception of the stakes involved, could create distinctly different results. Was it, as Usher once wrote to Lane, the "implied obligation" of the government to make provision for railroad companies to obtain perfect title to Indian lands? Or to guarantee a certain type of settlement pattern, or a certain degree of potential profit from timber cutting? Or was it the government's job to consider the Indian understanding of treaties "without regard to verbal quibbles" in terms of the railroads' interests? Must men react in a certain way to their economic environment? Is every attempt at a unique solution to a common predicament doomed to failure at the hands of the bureaucratic traditionalists? The study of Indian policy in Kansas prompts a hesitant "not necessarily." To this, however, it must be added that the factors which occasionally led to railroad defeat—the Potawatomi incident, the failure of the railroads to partition the Sac and Fox lands and, later, the Osage reserve—were not unrelated to the very elements for which the success of these companies might have been condemned.[20]

The mixed motives among reformers may be illustrated by examining the railroad-timber operation upon the Kickapoo reserve, which was described by the author of a careful tribal history as "a sordid chronicle of man's inhumanity to man." The Kickapoo tribe was perhaps better equipped to resist some of the promotional strategy of the railroads due to its experience with attempting to regulate roads and toll bridges in the 1850s. In December, 1857, the tribe filed a complaint in Washington that whites, without their consent, were traveling through their country on the Fort Leavenworth to Fort Kearney military road and the new road from Atchison to Vermillion City, and that they were spreading disease among the Indians. Not only was no compensation for damages offered the tribe, but one builder had gone so far as to demand that the Kickapoos fence his road with their own timber, citing a territorial statute as justification. Several toll bridges were erected over Grasshopper Creek, one by Ben Holladay, the famous freighter. The tribe complained that these bridges were becoming an excuse, not only for increased white travel but for white settlement. As was true of railroads later, the toll bridge people stated that they were obligated to erect dwellings, plant gardens, and maybe even construct a mail station in connection with their business. Given the existence of the roads and the refusal of the military to stop travel over the Kickapoo lands, some sort of regulated bridge did make sense. Kickapoo agent W. P. Badger negotiated bridge contracts in 1859 which provided that the privilege should last three years only, that Indians and Indian Office employees should have free use of the bridges, and that tolls should be set high to discourage casual travel. In the absence of bridges travelers tended to gather at the crossings at times when the streams were impassable. While waiting for the water to subside they helped themselves to the timber for firewood or for rafts or temporary bridges. Badger had first inquired of the Indian Office whether the Indians themselves could not construct toll bridges and pay for them out of their annuity funds. This reasonable possibility was vetoed in Washington, so the regulated franchise to private contractors emerged. Immediately, the bridge men objected, arguing that $2,000 invested in bridges could not be justified when limits were placed on their enterprise. One of them abandoned his operation in disgust in 1860 because of the regulations and because people so often forded the creek and waved at him on the way by the tollgate. The point is that the Kickapoos protected their interests as they saw them, which they as landholders had the right to do. It was then up to the white businessman to determine if he could make a profit on his Indian reserve business operation without speculating upon the misfortune of a traditional culture. Toll bridges, railroads, and timber companies might have been assets to Indian Kansas if their operators had conserved natural resources and kept the best interests of the Indians in mind. Such operations might have made possible a reasonable industrialization of the area while it was still under Indian control, thus eliminating much of the pressure for tribal removal. Enterprises directly run by the Indians or run by contractors answerable directly to the Indians might have been another means to this end. Neither set of possibilities was pursued with sincerity— direct Indian control, not at all.[21]

Perhaps because of this anomaly, the railroad purchase clause of the Kickapoo treaty of 1862 was drawn up by Samuel Pomeroy, United States senator and a major investor in the Atchison & Pike's Peak railroad, the beneficiary of the treaty's railroad sale clause. Agent Charles Keith presented to the tribe the standard agreement authorizing allotments to the Indians and sale of the surplus (123,832 acres) to the railroad at $1.25 per acre. Bonds could be issued for payment and no payment need be made to the tribe for seven years, thus providing quick profit with no liability.[22]

The reformers countered immediately with complaints of fraud, partly for the reasons given above and partly because rival railroad companies insisting on the privilege for themselves stirred up dissatisfaction among the already untrusting Kickapoos. When the treaty was ratified in 1863, some of the Kickapoos reported that they thought it was still in the negotiation stage. At the time of the negotiations a year earlier a Kansas grand jury had made an abortive investigation of Keith's role in the matter. In May, 1863, Commissioner William Dole himself journeyed to Kansas to appraise the situation, especially affairs related to the Kickapoo agency. He learned from those in control that the

Indians had not, at the time of negotiations, understood the interpreter, Paschal Pensioneau, who was regarded by at least some as closer to the railroad interests than his own tribe. Officials at the agency refused to answer a question as to whether they had promises of land from Pomeroy in return for influencing the Indians, but they were quick to point out that those who were charging fraud were in the pay of people from St. Joseph, Missouri, who wanted the lands for the Elmwood & Marysville railroad company. Keith denied that any of the Indians were drinking at the time of the treaty negotiations, and that he threatened them with military force if they did not sign. He did admit that he made some changes in the leadership of the Kickapoo tribe, including appointing Black Thunder, one of the principal signers of the treaty of 1862, as chief in 1861. Keith argued that no agent could keep his wards in a state of "subordination" if he did not have the power to dislodge traditional chiefs who might become "unruly."[23]

Others told a different story. John Anderson, who spoke Kickapoo and had taken No-cost-Ke-ah-quak and Pa-shaw-quaw to Topeka to complain to the United States court, said that Keith had threatened to withhold money appropriated to the tribe unless they signed, and that only six Kickapoos, elevated by Keith to positions of power against the will of the tribe, were willing to sell tribal lands to the railroad. According to one witness, only Pah-kah-hoh among all the signers of the treaty was a man respected by the tribe as a headman. Stephen Pensioneau was the son of the interpreter; Wah-mah-sher-baw was his wife; and the others were "the most trifling and worthless of the Kickapoos," including one child only ten years of age. Keith; Keith's brother-in-law; former agent Badger; L. C. Challis, president of the railroad; H. Terrill; and E. N. Knapp were said to have bribed key figures. Keith was reported to have exercised further influence through his ownership of the only store authorized to operate on the reserve. On the basis of this the Kansas attorney general, W. W. Guthrie, ordered the treaty suspended and the survey of the reserve stopped pending further investigation. Keith responded with the assertion that Guthrie was in the employ of the St. Joseph railroad clique which was determined to drive out both Keith and the Atchison & Pike's Peak railroad in order to replace them with its own set of officials and its own railroad. Obviously, the Indians were pawns in the scheme.[24]

So tainted were both sides with secret political and economic connections that it mattered little to the dissatisfied Indians whether the "reformers" won or not. The treaty was put into effect as written, without further investigation by either Congress or the executive branch. Edmund Ross charged in 1872 that the Pomeroy family got over 50,000 acres of Kickapoo land and that Keith and his wife had received 3,000 acres. A full section was conveyed for $1.00 to Elizabeth Dole, wife of the commissioner of Indian Affairs.[25]

The aftermath was typical. Before the railroad earned title to the lands through actual construction as specified in the treaty (fifteen miles within three years and completion through the reserve in three more) the timber problem arose once again. A new agent, F. G. Adams, furnished the district court in Topeka with subpoenas for witnesses in timber-stealing cases but found that the law was too defective on the matter to get convictions. He then tried to collect from individual offenders who had built the town of Hiawatha (ironically, a name that evokes a poetic image hardly in keeping with the ethics of the founders) from stolen Kickapoo timber. Settlers, disappointed with the grant to the railroad and consequent high land prices, decided that it was their right to take timber freely. Meanwhile, the railroad attempted to cut and sell the wood for its own benefit before the settlers helped themselves. In 1866 it also demanded the privilege of building a sawmill on a 640-acre tract reserved by treaty for the Kickapoos for the same purpose, but which the Indians had not utilized. At the same time, other railroads, such as the Atlantic & Pacific, were investing in scrip based on the profits from Kickapoo lands and offered for sale through Samuel E. Pomeroy. Adams did collect some compensation for timber damage, but, as in the case of Bartling on the

Delaware reserve, he did so by resorting on his own initiative to extra-legal measures after the complete failure of regular channels.[26]

Given the roundabout course taken by appeals to higher authority, it is not surprising that on occasion individual Indians took direct action against timber depredators and railroad fraud. That there was not widespread violence suggests psychological reasons for Indian docility that parallel the reasons advanced by Stanley Elkins and Winthrop Jordan to explain the passivity of black slaves and Jewish concentration camp inmates. Also, of course, there is the more practical explanation of intertribal confusion regarding paramount interests at stake.[27]

Perhaps the best example of direct action was in the Shawnee reserve. The Shawnees in the late fifties were upset with their agent for not protecting them against intruders. Their principal chief, Samuel Parks, himself aware of the game and motivated to protect tribal rights by plans of his own for self-enrichment, apparently was not wholly candid with his followers. Samuel Cormatzter, the Shawnee council clerk, wrote a witty letter to Secretary of the Interior Jacob Thompson in 1858, describing the Shawnee's annoyance at the rule of law as communicated by their agent:

> And when we do have one [an agent] and go to him for advice about something as apt as any way he will say well I will consult Mr. such an one in reference to your request. So he will hoist himself upon his dignity stilts and leave us. Well the next time we see him and ask about it he will tell us some unmeaning or some kind of excuse. Probably it is now too late. All the Agents we have had for the last 18 years are or have been better judges of Brandy than their duty I think.

Cormatzter reported that several Shawnees had been killed trying to protect the timber, and that the settler openly scoffed at the idea of an Indian suing him, especially since the tribe had never gotten the results of a survey from the Indian

Office to show the exact tracts which had been allotted to individuals according to their 1854 treaty. Soon after, their agent wrote that as a result of this trouble a group of young Shawnees in June, 1858, burned the houses of the squatters in the vicinity of the place where an Indian had been killed. Thus ended "intrusion" into the region. However, the agent hoped something less drastic could be devised. Nothing new happened. The Shawnees resorted to no more violence, while the standing timber continued to diminish.[28]

There were a few other alternative ways the Indians might foil the Indian ring and gain control of the capitalization of nature or at least effect a compromise. One was to grant timber-cutting privileges to a single contractor in hopes that he could be held responsible by the tribe and would prevent indiscriminate cutting. The Sac and Fox tribe attempted this and selected as their benefactor R. S. Stevens. However, Stevens regarded the contract as part of his larger operations, which included house building, railroad building, and other timber-intensive industries upon the various Indian reserves. He built a $1,000 sawmill on the Sac and Fox lands in 1860 and charged it to the Indian Department, claiming that it was needed to fulfill his contract to provide decent housing for the tribe. The Indians countered with the argument that they hardly needed a mill with a forty-horsepower steam engine, and charged that Stevens had a deal to sell wood to merchants, bankers, and mechanics in Lawrence at a personal profit. The houses he built were shoddy, the timber was cut in wholesale quantities, and the charge for houses was estimated at 20 percent more than the work was worth. Still, the general policy on the Sac and Fox lands was to grant contracts to a "better class" of whites, which their agent in 1862 said "worked about as well as anything"—that is to say, not very well at all. A second possibility was to make intratribal rules against anyone in the tribe selling timber. The Potawatomis attempted this in 1866, but it was impossible to enforce for the simple reason that no tribal unanimity about the threat could be reached. Last, the tribes could continue to hope for federal legislation on Indian timber. George Manypenny in 1856 found only one piece of legislation which could be used: a March, 1831, act entitled "An act to provide for the punishment of offenses committed in cutting destroying &c Live Oak and other timber or trees reserved for naval purposes." Neither the 1807 act to prevent settlement on Indian land nor the Trade and Intercourse Act of 1834 made any specific mention of timber. That no better legislation was passed represents a serious oversight by friends of justice to the Indian.[29]

It must be concluded that the capitalization of nature through the building of railroads and the cutting of timber met with few checks, so thoroughly did the idea appeal to the men involved in subverting the Indians and their protectors. The common law adjusted in expected fashion, the executive bureaucracy pursued its duty only so far as the welcoming arms of the Indian ring embraced it, and the tribes were so split and jaded by the process as to find it difficult to sort out where their interests lay. In short, the devices worked, and they worked through a combination of complexity, apathy, and corruption. In retrospect it is obvious that, far from being purposely sinister, the outcome was wholly American. Public-domain historians point with outrage at the disregard of the public interest by government and entrepreneur alike in exploiting coal, timber, and metals on non-Indian lands and at the failure to guard the people's equity in opening natural resources to private development. One of them, Thomas Le Duc, has noted that "Americans seem to have felt a greater need for ritualistic declaration of a moral code than for achieving even minimal adherence to it. Why this was so I must leave to the cultural anthropologists." The government in this case did nothing to the Indians it did not do to its own citizens. It failed to protect timber until railroads earned their "fair" land patents, it failed to move decisively upon forfeiture and other provisions of the carefully drawn treaties. But the executive bureaucracy allowed distortion of the intent of these treaties no more than it did of the laws of Congress applicable to the nation at large.[30]

That of course does not make Indian policy palatable,

The End of Indian Kansas

nor does it soften the repulsiveness of it in the abstract. As early as 1858 it was reported that in the Neosho agency, where several small tribes resided, attitudes toward the natural resource base of recent Indian communal wealth were so thoroughly transformed that settlers were prohibiting Indians from cutting any timber. The unfortunate Indians were forced to pick up sticks which had fallen naturally to the ground, while the settlers were threatening to kill the Indians attempting to improve their homes. Several natives were severely beaten and threatened with death for planting crops. The agent had no authority to call troops without authorization from Washington, where ambitious politicos were sorting out their Kansas-based portfolios. These men discounted reports that some tribes were purposefully setting prairie fires in Kansas. After all, it was assumed that those on both sides of the question were nothing if not practical men.[31]

CHAPTER THREE

The Indian Ring

IT HAS BEEN SUGGESTED that, regardless of formal laws and treaties, the impact of personality upon Indian affairs in Kansas was overwhelming. The Indians there were neither a sovereign nation nor a conquered enemy, but rather were wards whose riches were to be held in trust by guardians in what was defined by these guardians as the wards' best interest. The effectiveness of this trust system depended on the economics and ethics of its execution, and this in turn rested upon the perceptions and priorities of government officials as well as the contractors to whom fell the ultimate decision about the handling of the trust. Unfortunately, the temptation to divert large accumulations of capital that rightfully belonged to Indians to other than Indian use was often greater than the strength of individual consciences. After all, capital was scarce in the West, and Indian money—accumulated from congressional appropriations or from trust funds from land sales—could be used as an indirect government subsidy to western enterprise while at the same time presenting the illusion that the tribes were being fairly treated.

A sort of "black legend" grew up concerning the administration of Indian trust funds. It was often charged, without being very specific, that there existed an "Indian ring"—a combination of federal officials and businessmen allied in a conspiracy to defraud both the Indians and the United States government by turning the whole philanthropic intent of Indian policy to its own selfish ends. Just after Kansas Territory was created, the 1855 congressional debate on the Indian appropriation bill centered on this issue. Congressmen were unsure whether the trust funds should be invested in state stocks or railroad bonds or "in all kinds of reckless schemes for persons who are dependent on us for the fidelity with which they are administered." One senator expressed strong indignation because Indian contractors and white attorneys were infiltrating the tribes and making unregulated bargains with them concerning their funds. He continued:

> I would do no wrong to the red man; and I would, least of all, while I was pretending to civilize, to christianize, and to elevate him to the standard of the white man, teach him first to be a robber, a knave, a swindler, and an ingrate, as our government does by its policy . . . . You speak to them with the voice of Jacob while you give to them the hairy hand of Esau. Sir, what morals can you expect from such teachers?

Ten years later the core of the Indian appropriation bill debate was that things had gotten so out of hand that the government might as well bring all the Indians to the Astor House in New York and support them as to pay the expenses of the Indian ring. In 1863 General James Blunt wrote to Washington from Kansas asking that a special agent be sent out to investigate Indian matters in the state. He specifically warned that this must be an honest man "who is not interested in Indian contracts and engaged in robbing them of what is left them by the rebels." Four years later, the *Leavenworth Conservative* complained bitterly that this Indian ring had made a "ridiculous farce" of the highly significant treaty conferences at Medicine Lodge. To Indian agents, traders, and "the whole brood of thieves who fatten upon the spoils of a system more false in theory than ruinous and rotten in practice," the newspaper threatened, "we shall denounce you until you reform or have your claws drawn."[1]

Suspicion of civilian profit motives in handling Indian affairs in Kansas no doubt contributed a great deal to early exchanges leading to the great transfer question in 1876. Because many came to believe both that the Indian Department was "a systematic swindle, out of which a small army of speculators are making fortunes," and that the Indians were so degraded that "only their passions direct their beast-like minds," there was a great deal of sentiment for transferring control of Indian affairs from the Interior Department to the War Department, where it had been prior to 1849. The opinion was expressed in Kansas that parleying with the Indians benefited mainly the Indian ring, and that dictating to them through military force was a more humane as well as a more efficient system. This lack of confidence made the job of well-intentioned Interior Department officials difficult. George Clarke, the Potawatomi agent, wrote in his 1855 report, "I am of the unchangeable opinion that government should not only *assume* the patriarchial, but *exercise* a dictatorial rule over this tribe." So entrenched was the Indian ring and so helpless were the Indians, said Clarke, that it would be "better by far . . . were they to receive all their improvement fund in *telescopes* . . . never to be used or understood, than that the fund be paid them in money at annual payments." There seemed to be, he continued, a "higher law" party in Kansas Territory, which included notables from the governor on down who were not interested in a strict interpretation of laws regarding Indians.[2]

The elements of the ring, it should be emphasized, did not necessarily coalesce completely on every issue, nor were such individuals as Pomeroy, Stevens, or Ewing able in every situation to control its disparate parts. To complete the ring, it was necessary that at least five factions be in substantial agreement: those in control at the Indian Office in Washington, opinion leaders on Indian affairs in Congress, the agent of the tribe involved, businessmen who stood to benefit from a particular set of actions, and at least a part of the tribal leadership. Which of these elements was most important, whether all of them fell in line, or whether all of them were needed depended upon the precise situation. Often the ring operated with some of its elements missing, which usually resulted in an investigation and unwelcome publicity and led to only partial success or to dismal failure of the operation. For example, in the 1862 Kickapoo treaty, the Indian leaders were not completely informed (with the exception of Pensioneau, the interpreter) and they raised an awkward fuss, as did certain agency employees who did not subscribe to Keith's tactics. Pomeroy, representing both Congress and the business interest, and Dole in the Indian Office (who served as the investigator) were in agreement, however, and the scheme could stand on these three legs. In the case of the Potawatomi railroad attempt, the agent was missing from the ring. He carried out the allotment of lands to Indians who then were not yet split, as they would later be, into factions upon which the ring could obtain more leverage. In this case, despite the attempted coordination of the other elements, the ring was too crippled to work, and the U.P.E.D. ultimately declined its option.

It is mostly in cases where the ring functioned less than perfectly that the historian has information to study, because when things ran smoothly the charges and investigations which exposed some of the structure were not recorded. However, the ring often did not operate smoothly, for it was not a preconceived or permanent conspiratorial structure, but rather one which recreated itself in slightly different form as each challenge arose, and as the various interests gathered about it. In some cases an element might be omitted without affecting the success of the operation. For example, Congress, which was far removed from the day-to-day setting where the ring thrived, might not be involved. Usually the impetus for creating the ring arose first with the businessmen, who often experienced damaging internal factionalism. An example from material already presented would be the Kickapoo schemers who were shaken by support for defeat of the treaty from a rival St. Joseph, Missouri, railroad corporation. In fact, it appeared that another ring was in the formative stages and wished to replace Keith with its own man, as well as to use such public officials as W. W. Guthrie to further its end. There could also be complex fractures within other elements which have been broadly described here. The agency employees could fail to follow the lead of the agent, as happened with the Kickapoos. The central superintendent, who enjoyed administrative control of all Indian agencies in Kansas, might get wind of something at the agency level and throw a wrench in the works, as Superintendent Thomas Murphy often did. Or for that matter, a split might develop at the superintendent's level, as, for example, when Murphy's chief clerk, Thomas Lawler, made serious charges against Murphy and started an investigation of this office as it impinged on ring activities. While the theme may on first glance appear coherent, there were infinite variations and gradations, with the result that any attempt to describe the ring's role in Indian dispossession is bound to appear somewhat oversimplified. Therefore, to discern the complexity of the matter it is best to plunge into the dynamics of specific cases, both here and, less directly, in later chapters.

As pointed out in a recent study of Indian administration on the frontier, the Indian agents, due to a lack of communication from Washington, were often placed in the position of having wide discretion not only in executing but in determining policy, while at the same time finding themselves subjected to the most extreme pressures. Certainly, a look at the agents in Kansas during the period 1854–1870 indicates that any assessment of their moral responsibility for what the ring was able to accomplish there must take into account the effects of the harrowing circumstances in which they were placed. Living either off the reservation in nearby towns or in many cases in ramshackle buildings at the agency itself, they were subjected to extreme physical and mental tension. During the territorial troubles of the late 1850s Agent William Gay of the Shawnees was killed on the road to Westport carrying Indian monies, and his son was badly wounded, after which those operating the Shawnee Mission fled the territory in terror. Agent Montgomery of the Kansas was arrested by local authorities on an arson charge after he had burned twenty squatter cabins illegally located on Kaw lands near Topeka. Agent Clarke of the Potawatomis and his family were threatened by over a thousand armed outlaws marauding in the region of his isolated house. Obtaining instructions from Washington or reasonable protection was extremely difficult. Most agents in Kansas did not have copies of the statutes relating to Indian affairs nor the Indian Department rules, though they received circulars from Washington from time to time. The Neosho agent noted as late as 1867 that it took from ten to forty-five days for letters to get from Fort Smith, Arkansas, where the southern superintendency office was located, to his office at Baldwin City, Kansas.[3]

Often the threat to the physical security of the agent would grow out of disagreement regarding the way he had carried out his responsibilities. Since he could expect little aid from Washington, he perhaps was driven to establish local connections in order to avoid the oft-repeated spectacle of an agent being driven out of office by local businessmen posing for the moment as nightriders. Whether the agent cooperated or was forced seemed not to make a great deal of difference. Something, however, should have been done about situations like that on the Osage reserve in 1867, when settlers tried to hang the agent, and the military refused to intervene. In fact, so dangerous were the circumstances that two Friends who visited the Kansas tribes in 1868 asked the Indian Office for protection, not from the Indians but from troops stationed in the district.[4]

An agent who cooperated with the local ring of white settlers and businessmen ran the risk of running into trouble with the Indians, but of the two the Indian was often considered the less dangerous. In 1865 the tribes on the Great Nemaha reserve attempted to murder their agent, whom they believed had swindled them out of $4,000 and had acted in concert with local whites to dupe them into selling their lands. They forced the agent, Major John A. Burbank, to open the safe in his office so that they could personally examine the records, and when Burbank fled to his house to get a gun they fired several shots at him. Burbank then called the cavalry, who quickly responded, as it probably would not have if the complaint had been directed against whites. Nine Indians were arrested.[5]

Another example of Indian pressure upon an agent in 1870 was considerably more subtle. Albert Wiley, agent for the Sacs and Foxes, was unpopular with the tribe because he was involved with a ring. He was a partner in the real-estate firm of Craig and Wiley at Quenemo, Kansas, which was interested in buying Sac and Fox lands, and he had been recommended as agent on political grounds by a former agent, Perry Fuller, whose appointment, as shall be seen, was a notorious example of ring efficiency. In 1870 Chief Keokuk of the Sac and Fox tribe hired an attorney, James Christian, to defend him against a suit by James Wiley, brought to vindicate the agent's action in forcibly restraining Keokuk from going to Washington and holding him on the reservation. The precise circumstances under which this very unusual lawsuit was brought are unknown, but, in any case, the brief of Keokuk's attorney read more like a prosecution than a defense. He argued that the Indian Office did not have the power to order assault, battery, and imprisonment of Indians even though it might have rules about Indians leaving the reservation for Washington. As for treaties between the tribes and the government, they were couched in the language of equals:

> Have we abandoned the principle of treating this people with justice and humanity, of refusing them the blessings of civilization and Christianity; if so, where is our boasted civilization, where our vaunted progress? If civilized and intelligent men, like my client, are to be restrained of their natural liberty,

and confined to the narrow limits of their now "Diminished Reserves," compelled to associate with none other than Indian agents, Indian traders, and their pimps and strikers, I don't think they would learn much civilization and refinement, and less Christianity, for as a class these men have never been accused of over-refined notions of either honesty or morals.

To say that no delegation of Indians could come to Washington was, according to Christian, nothing more than slavery, and as a practical matter the situation resulted in servitude to the Indian ring. Wiley, it was charged, was a corrupt agent. He was in league with the reserve trader and had threatened to remove those chiefs who were distasteful to him, including Keokuk. Though this same Moses Keokuk, being the head of the "progressive" section of the tribe, probably was involved in as many schemes to defraud his people as the agent could have been, that was not really the issue of the litigation. Christian portrayed a "yelling pack of human bloodhounds" pursuing the Indian. "The army must be sent in," he concluded in a mock prediction of the final assault, "to protect the harmless and innocent creature, the professional squatter, who is so meek and inoffensive that he would not trespass on the rights of even an Indian; contracts must then be let to supply the army to white speculators; money must be made, even if it is at the expense of blood—but it is only Indian blood. Their lands are more desirable than their lives." Christian's last statement lacked no irony, especially if one interprets "lives" to mean lives remotely related to what the majority of the tribe had once known and wished.[6]

Miscellaneous charges against agents were very common, and many involved either suspected collusion with the Indian ring or complaints by the ring against an agent who displeased its members. In 1853 George Ewing, one of the largest operators in the Indian trade, cultivated his understanding with the "progressive" faction of the Sac and Fox tribe at the expense of the agent. He protested that Thomas Connally, a half-breed, had been treated roughly by Agent John Chenault, and he argued eloquently that this was a sovereign nation unworthy of such malice. Connally added that Chenault "feels his dignity a great deal more than President Pierce does his" and hoped that a change of administration in Washington would come soon and so end the term of many Kansas agents. The result of such pressure by Ewing was that Chenault was replaced by Burton James. Yet while James, called by Ewing a "worthy citizen of Missouri," seemed to satisfy the ring, he was anathema to much of the tribe. In March, 1857, the complaint was voiced that James, far from having more respect for tribal sovereignty than Chenault, took upon himself the right to appoint chiefs and to pay them a $500 salary to keep them loyal to him. He employed an interpreter of "a mongrel Band from some other nation," who distorted important matters in translation and who did not allow other bilingual Indians on the reservation. He had, the tribe charged, driven off all traders except a few (Ewing, for example) chosen by him, and it was rumored that he had direct financial interests in the trade. James operated a butcher shop, and he was charged with withholding just payments in business transactions. He was said to be so addicted to gambling that he could not take time off to see the headmen and chiefs. He also owned a large farm and ranch in the country nearby. Indians charged that he allowed outsiders to come into the reserve to graze stock and to harvest timber. It was said that he personally whipped and beat some of the Sac and Fox headmen for trivial offenses. Other agents charged with being in collusion with traders included Luke Lea of the Potawatomis, in 1859, and Henry Martin of the Sacs and Foxes, in 1866. Martin was charged with failing to distribute annuities properly and with being in the pay of the trading firm of (Thomas) Carney and (Robert S.) Stevens of Leavennworth. Mo-ko-ho-ko, the chief of the intransigent full-blood faction, said at that time that Keokuk, who earlier attacked James and was later so vehemently against Wiley, was part of the ring as it existed at that time and that he journeyed to Washington to defend Martin.[7]

In the case of the Sac and Fox agency in the late fifties, several more elements were added to trader collusion, with the result that a more efficiently operating ring appeared. In 1858 Agent Francis Tymany complained of being literally terrorized by what came to be known as the "Centrapolis gang," of which Perry Fuller was the head. Orphaned at an early age, Fuller had gone to work with the trading firm of Northrup and Chick. Later he took a claim at the little town of Centrapolis, eight miles north of the Sac and Fox reserve, and sold $40,000 worth of goods from his consignment store and trading operation in the first year. Tymany, however, came to the conclusion concerning Centrapolis that "the worst men reside there that ever figured in the annals of crime," and he tried to turn the trade of his wards away from those "sinks of sorrow and shame" to the north. As a result, Fuller tampered with the Sac and Fox chiefs with the objective of eroding the agent's influence. He also used considerable political power in the area against Tymany and hired ruffians to threaten officials at the annuity payments, thus openly revealing motives which Tymany said were "of the most corrupt and dangerous kind." Many Sacs and Foxes were dying from poisoned liquor acquired from the Centrapolis gang, and their symptoms of bleeding from the mouth or vomiting led Tymany to believe that the brew contained strychnine.[8]

The Centrapolis-based ring was much too strong and well connected for Tymany. Both Tymany and his predecessor, Burton James, asked for military force to stop the "combination of wicked and depraved white men" who were stealing timber and horses on the reserve and taking the former commodity to a sawmill in town owned and operated by Perry Fuller. The governor of Kansas Territory, James W. Denver, refused to provide this force, explaining that he did not have sufficient men. He said the courts in that district were too corrupted by the ring to convict these men, and even if they were convicted there were no prisons to hold them. Also, the governor argued, the problem was the responsibility of the Indian Office. Meanwhile, the ring timber agent informed Tymany that if he tried to stop the cutting he could be killed; a rifle was pointed at the agent to substantiate the threat. Fuller was as successful in lobbying with territorial officials as Tymany was unsuccessful. Several marshals came to the agency to arrest a man on what both Tymany and James insisted were trumped-up charges. When Tymany objected he was arrested for "obstructing of justice." This was quickly followed by the replacement of Tymany as agent by the Indian Office, only a little more than a year after his appointment. The new agent was Perry Fuller.[9]

The Fuller case well illustrates the complexity of evaluating the role of the agent in the West in oversimplified terms, and the danger (given the present stage of research) of being too confident in assigning virtue or vice to groups rather than individuals. Fuller was charged by the Chippewas in 1859 with supporting white men who had married into the tribe for the purpose of defrauding it, and with encouraging speculation in the Indian domain so that speculators fought with each other over the spoils. As late as 1866, Fuller still claimed to be the attorney for the Sacs and Foxes, which the principal chief denied. Later, he purchased 5,438 acres of the tribe's reserve, probably with ring profits. At the end of the Civil War Perry Fuller & Company had moved to bigger and better things. He had become one of the largest contractors supplying the Navajos and other southwestern tribes.[10]

Given the intense speculation upon the strategically situated Delaware lands, which were some of the first to be sold, it is little wonder that questions concerning the role of the agent also arose there. In 1862 the tribe demanded the removal of Agent Fielding Johnson and the expulsion of Carney and Stevens as mercantile operators on the Delaware reserve. Johnson, it was reported, had lost the respect of the tribe due to his repeated "cursing of the Indians and threatening them with the contents of his revolver." He had been a trader before his appointment as agent, and the leaders of the tribe were convinced that he had established business connections which had assured his appointment, and to which he was beholden as agent. He had shot at least one Indian under circumstances which might have been avoided, and he was also charged with consorting with Silas Armstrong, a Wyandot tribal citizen who played the same role that Abelard Guthrie did among the Shawnees or Moses Keokuk among the Sacs and Foxes. Armstrong had taken the guardianship of many Wyandot children then living with the rest of the tribe among the Delawares and was widely hated by members of the tribe for denying these children their just dues while he himself lived in luxury in Washington, D. C. So suspicious did the tribe become that even John Pratt, a long-time Baptist missionary among the Delawares who succeeded Johnson, sought the aid of Senator Pomeroy in defending himself from accusations that he was speculating with Delaware funds.[11]

Johnson did defend himself, saying that he was being threatened with assassination by irresponsible Indians who wished to discredit him for selfish reasons. One of Johnson's friends said that he was under attack by outside interests who considered him too scrupulous. In fact, since most of the charges against Johnson stemmed from his high temper (which might be charitably described as righteous indignation) rather than from his collusion with whites, there may have been emerging here the not uncommon pattern of an agent being forced out by a ring which simply could not corrupt him. Johnson's friend said he would ride for days looking for lost Delaware stock and would give money to destitute Indians from his own pocket. A witness to the shooting for which Johnson was criticized said that it involved a drunken Delaware named Jim Harrison, who was imbibing from a quart canteen and passing it around. Johnson asked him for the canteen, since liquor was not allowed on Indian reserves, but was refused. The agent then ordered two soldiers to seize it, whereupon Harrison pulled a knife and rushed them. The soldiers requested permission to fire, but the agent refused. Ten additional soldiers immediately surrounded the Indian with fixed bayonets. Harrison drew his tomahawk and Johnson stepped into the circle. The Indian then rushed him with the tomahawk and knife; the agent backed off and ordered the solders to hit the Indian with the butts of their rifles and knock him down. In the ensuing struggle the head of one soldier was split with the tomahawk. Johnson finally shot Harrison, wounding but not fatally injuring him. Johnson may well have lacked tact, but that he attempted to act in what he conceived to be the interests of the Indians at the time seems apparent although not absolutely certain.[12]

In such cases it is difficult to tell whether the agent was villain or victim, or whether he represented a ring or was being attacked by one. It is likewise often difficult to determine for certain whether Indian funds which were diverted from their intended use were diverted by a ring, by individual greed on the part of an agent, by well-intentioned adjustments in the field, or by innocent carelessness. On the shallow edge of the pro-agent position is the case of Clinton C. Hutchinson, first Sac and Fox agent and later special agent for the Ottawas. Hutchinson was a major architect of a plan to provide the Ottawas with a university. When his accounts came up short by over $40,000 he argued that he had invested the money in a university building for the benefit of the tribe, even though not necessarily in the manner for which the money was originally appropriated. After three mistrials in the federal courts for fraud, Hutchinson finally settled with the Treasury Department in an out-of-court agreement for $1,000. He had a receipt which he had gotten from the tribal council (by what means was the subject of considerable debate), exonerating him from responsibility for the money. In fact, long before this incident Hutchinson had been in trouble for the diversion of other public funds. He was dismissed from his position as agent for the unfortunate Sacs and Foxes in 1862, for authorizing them to borrow $2,000 for a trip to Washington without approval from his Indian Office superiors. Though Usher then concluded that Hutchinson was clearly "not a proper person to be Indian agent," he was quickly reinstated in the Indian service as agent for the Ottawas, who, by provisions in their 1862 treaty for a school to be funded by sale of their land, had created a responsibility for their trustees greater than any other in Kansas. He was constantly trying to account for disappearing funds, even to the point of swearing that a large sum for which he could not account was destroyed in a bank fire during William Quantrill's famous raid on Lawrence in 1863.[13]

Quantrill's raid figured more believably in the difficulties of a Shawnee agent, James Abbott, who was criticized by several tribes in his arena of operation for inducing the Quapaws and others to sign illicit leases on their lands. Abbott went to Lawrence with his own team, taking with him $900 belonging to the Shawnees in hopes of depositing it at a safer place than the agency safe. The following morning Quantrill made his infamous raid. The burning of the stable destroyed Abbott's $225 carriage, his horses, and his valise. While running from the Eldridge House to escape, the agent ran through a hog yard. In scrambling over the fence, he dropped his pocketbook containing the money. After the raid he returned, only to discover that the hogs had chewed up the case and scattered currency all over the yard. Abbott recovered all but $70, probably fully appreciative of the fact that it was not only the Indian ring that was hoggish when it came to Indian funds.[14]

Obviously the stakes were highest for the various rings, the agents, and the Indians during the time that a treaty was being negotiated. Agents were beset by potential buyers of land on the one hand, the Indians were interested in income and land titles on the other, while traders appeared in the wings to make sure the treaty took care of them. Contractors were interested in surveying jobs, while gifts were distributed to chiefs who little understood that these were sometimes being paid out of the tribe's own government-protected trust fund.[15]

Prominent among those in attendance and especially

active at the treaty negotiations were the traders. Since they usually had claims against the tribe, they were in a unique position to manipulate the Indians to their own advantage. In some instances the Indian Office suggested the use of an order system whereby Indians wishing to buy something would apply to the agent for an order on the next annuity. If the agent determined that he needed the goods, the Indian took the order to an authorized trader who would take it in place of cash. Settlement would be made at the next annuity payment between the agent and the several traders licensed by him. In this way large amounts of cash were not floating about, and the number of traders was limited; but the system got out of hand as quickly as any other, and the tribes soon found themselves overextended. Sometimes attempts were made to make sure the Indians did not trade on credit at all, but this was in fact impossible to enforce. Even when the order system was in full operation, traders often gave the Indian credit without getting an order from the agent, and then appeared at the next treaty conference with substantial claims for individual Indian debts which were difficult for either the government or the tribal council to dispute.[16]

Probably the trader with the most influence was George Ewing, who brought to Kansas experience with immigrant tribes extending back to the removal tragedies of the 1830s. Upon his entrance into the trade in Kansas Territory, he protested to the Indian Office that the returns were terribly unprofitable, but the fact that he and his associates stuck with it for the next twenty years surely suggests that there were adequate compensations. In early 1854 he said that though he had been in Kansas for five years he found the trade "not only unprofitable, but a most disastrous business for me." He described the Indians as lazy and extravagant: "At payment, they of late fail to pay, or many pay in part, some pay nothing, and a great many die." Ewing sold his large store in Westport, Missouri, and tried to sell his $35,000 stock of Indian goods, including two thousand English blankets, to the Interior Department. He also gave

Commissioner Manypenny some advice about the negotiation of treaties then in progress, stating that if they were carried out along the lines of the treaties negotiated with these same tribes by Lewis Cass several decades earlier, things might look better for the traders. Given Ewing's later activities, things apparently took a change for the better (at least in his view) following passage of the Kansas-Nebraska Act.[17]

Three months later, complaints were coming to Washington from John Goodell about strong activity by the Ewing firm in attempting to influence treaty negotiations. Goodell, at the Sac and Fox agency in Kansas, advised Manypenny that he was confronted with a ring interested in keeping him quiet, and that when he had tried to voice complaints about the irresponsibility of the Ewing strategy, Burton James had driven him from his home. He wrote: "If exposing the imposition and by whom they are imposed upon is outlawry I see no chance to get along in the Indian Country but to be a scamp with the balance." Goodell said he was repeatedly charged with being against the Indians selling their lands, but he reassured the Washington office that he had no such unseemly views, and that he was only "against their selling it for the benefit of unprincipled men whether they are traders or others." At the Potawatomi agency the following year, complaints were again voiced about the Ewings, this time that they were taking advantage of the Indian attorney business. These attorneys combined with individuals within a tribe to have money due the tribe paid to them, and ultimately it went to the Ewing firm. The agent styled this as "corrupting, demoralizing, and productive of the most disastrous effects upon the Indians, and [it does] more to counteract the benevolent intentions and wise policy of the government than any other cause that now exists." Later, in 1855, the Potawatomi chiefs expressed delight at the prospect that their treaty negotiations might be pursued in Washington rather than in Indian country, where Ewing would run the show. They said that only prompt intervention by the Indian Department could prevent the execution of a "hellish design" whereby Ewing and several half-breeds would pocket a large portion of the tribal annuities for years to come.[18]

Naturally, Ewing did not let this sort of talk go unchallenged. In fact it must be said that the effectiveness of his arguments, particularly in demonstrating to many Indians and much of the concerned public that his policy was no more dangerous than the designs of Congress and government clerks, accounted for his continued success. For example, when in 1855 Ewing obtained a power of attorney from the Potawatomis to prosecute their claims against the government for a fee of 50 percent of the awards, Manypenny termed the practice overt corruption, especially since Ewing was bribing the half-breeds and spreading unfounded rumors about the agent. George Clarke believed that Ewing was in league with Andrew Reeder, the territorial governor, and assured Washington that it was certain that "Mr. Ewing could counteract me with the crook of his finger." Ewing's defense of himself in this instance was printed in the *Annual Report of the Commissioner of Indian Affairs,* and so received relatively broad publicity. He stated that the Indian Office was trying to stop the appointment of attorneys by the tribes only because it was afraid that these attorneys would uncover corruption in Washington. The government attorneys were heartless, wrote Ewing, "yet these same *d——d hypocritical* scamps will skin a tribe out of a quarter or *half a million* of dollars at a lick, when they get a chance." Was it right, Ewing asked, to ignore treaties and to keep back money owed for over twenty years, as the government was demonstrably doing? Paradoxically, Ewing had a case, supporting the old adage that people who live in glass houses should not throw stones. He of course did nothing to justify his own methods, but he so thoroughly discredited his attackers that he ensured continued corruption rather than real reform.[19]

So confident was Ewing of his position that he took his case for claims against the Shawnees into a United States District Court in Missouri. In 1855 Richard Thompson and George Ewing filed suit against Joseph Parks and Black

Hoof, Shawnee chiefs, concerning a contract supposedly made with Thompson to pay him 20 percent of all annuities allowed the Shawnee chiefs under the seventh article of the 1831 treaty. Thompson had assigned half interest in this contract to Ewing. Later there was a supplemental agreement giving the two 50 percent of the proceeds from 100,000 acres of land sold by this article, in return for their services in prosecuting the claim of the Shawnees. That the tribe should have had any doubt about getting the money and should have found it necessary to contract with attorneys at such percentages spoke ill for the intent of the government to fulfill its treaty obligations quickly. Ewing and Thompson said they had obtained the tribes' promised treaty money only after a "terrible expense" of lobbying in Washington. The Shawnees had at last been paid $66,246.23 in July of 1853—money owed them for twenty years—but the cash was not paid in the East, since an act of August, 1852, had outlawed the usual practice of paying attorneys their cut in Washington before the money was distributed in Indian country. The Indians paid Ewing and Thompson only $6,340 and contended that the courts had no jurisdiction over the tribe. The case then was filed.[20]

The Shawnees hired A. J. Isaacs as their attorney, thus contracting another $5,000 debt for his fee. The Indian Office explored in detail the manner whereby the Indians had managed to make the contract with Ewing and Thompson in the first place, without the consent of the department, since there was a rule that all contracts not so approved were void. The Shawnees won the court case, but Ewing and Thompson threatened to appeal. At this point George Manypenny, no great friend of the Ewings', became enraged and contended that Chief Parks had gotten himself into trouble without authorization, and that it might be best to simply allow Parks and the trader to fight it out in the courts, while relieving the tribe as well as the Indian Office from all responsibility. The act of August 30, 1852, had stated not only that money appropriations were to be paid to the tribe per capita rather than through attorneys but that the executive

The End of Indian Kansas

department recognized no contract between Indian tribes and attorneys for the prosecution of claims. Thompson replied that the Indians had intended that he be paid and had tried to introduce this into their 1854 treaty, but they were prevented by the persistent interference of Manypenny, who probably had acted out of personal spite against the traders. The case was not appealed, but the attorneys did manage to use the threat of it to induce the Shawnees to vote them another $4,500.[21]

Sometimes the litigation moved in a different direction, as when the federal government sued Ewing in 1858 for $30,860 which was paid to him by the Potawatomi agent without authority. This was the reward for services rendered to ensure the payment of Potawatomi agricultural funds in cash rather than implements. The Indian Office, however, argued that Ewing's power of attorney from the Potawatomis, granted in 1852, was limited. He was not authorized to examine, as he did, all unpaid claims of that tribe from 1789 to 1852; nor was he authorized to collect more than one-third of the proceeds. The case faltered only because the testimony of the agent was not considered sufficient, and it was too expensive to collect affidavits.[22]

In the lucrative business of acting as Indian attorneys the roles of trader and contractor blurred, so that in fact both significant divisions of the business end of the Indian ring, the trader and the Indian contractor, sought to represent the tribe as attorney and thus to establish an extremely tight relationship. The negligence of the government and the audacity of the settlers made this a sustainable business. The Indians, who could not spend the necessary time in Washington to cultivate influence and to pursue the sometimes pointless legal maneuvers which were necessary to force the bureaucracy to pay them their just dues, had little choice but to depend upon men who might be defrauding them with one hand while saving them with the other. Certainly, some tribes, the Sacs and Foxes for instance, had their fair share of it. Wrote the *New York Times,* in 1868:

Everybody knows something of the Sacs and Foxes.

. . . Everybody does not know as much apparently of the leeching and plucking to which this tribe of red men has for years been subject thanks to the Indian bureau, Indian agents, & Indian traders. To make a long story short, it appeared that an "Indian ring" has fastened upon the confederate Sacs and Foxes & is immersed in the praiseworthy study of finding out how much it can secure & how little the Indians shall receive of their money.

These traders and attorneys did not lose their hold when Indian Kansas was finished. The heirs of C. N. Vann and William Adair, attorneys for the Osages in the 1865 and 1868 treaty negotiations, were still claiming fees when a congressional committee investigated that matter in 1905.[23]

One of the clearest examples of a ring involvement in the exploitation of Indian claims by contractors rather than traders was the case of the Shawnee depredation claims resulting from damage to their property by whites. James Abbott, who had experienced so much trouble with Indian funds and the hogs during the Quantrill raid, was told two years later that the money would be on its way to Kansas. He then received a letter from Edward Clark in Washington informing him that no money at the Treasury was available. The agent heard nothing more until Clark, styling himself as a Shawnee attorney, and Hall (presumably William A. Hall, a member of Congress), arrived in Kansas with a large chest of gold. Clark explained that after waiting about at the Treasury Department for two weeks he had learned that there were no funds available for the Shawnees, due to the expenses of the Civil War and the large number of other Indian claims. However, he convinced the clerks to pay in Treasury notes, which he collected on the tribe's behalf. He then contacted Hall and assigned him part of the 20 percent of the funds he expected as attorney, and the two borrowed an equivalent amount of gold, which they felt would be more acceptable to the Shawnees, keeping the notes themselves. Abbott was informed that they had just come from the Indian Office and were authorized to make settlements with the individual Indians for their claims. They were distinguished men, well connected in Washington, and they had with them very official-looking blanks to use as receipts. Abbott, therefore, allowed them to proceed, while he attended to other matters.[24]

It was not long before things went awry. Matthew King, whom Abbott sent with the pair as interpreter, and Paschal Fish, a Shawnee chief, told Abbott that the men were not wholly candid with the Indians regarding the deductions they were making from the money appropriated—the 20 percent attorneys' fee, 7.5 percent for the risk in borrowing the gold, and 10 percent for "extra services" Clark felt he had performed in getting the money. Fish reminded Clark that the tribe had loaned him money to travel to Washington when it had first appointed him as attorney, and that in fact he owed the tribe considerable money. King said that when meeting with the Indians Clark did the talking and Hall acted as banker. Even Hall was upset about the way Clark was negotiating, often settling with an Indian for much less than was his proper claim and pocketing the difference between that figure and the appropriated amount minus fees. Abbott then gave Clark a strong lecture on the reality of the matter, and things seemed to go better. However, when the two left rather suddenly the agent was not at all satisfied that all obligations had been met and demanded that they leave $1,000 to settle any discrepancies that might arise. Abbott soon discovered that the Shawnees had been swindled out of an amount he estimated at $10,000 and the Indian Office set at $18,000. The Indian Office took the position that it had authorized Abbott to pay the claims and disclaimed any knowledge of Clark and Hall. Thus the agent found himself charged with acting in collusion with the two and taking $1,000 in bribes. He was exonerated due to subsequent analysis of the circumstances and the support of Senator James Lane. How Clark obtained the notes from the Treasury Department without the cooperation of the agent or the knowledge of the Indian Office remains a mystery, thus obscuring the role of certain members of this ring who must have been crucial to its success.[25]

Clark and Hall were small fry among contractors compared to Robert S. Stevens. A native of New York State, Stevens became the most successful Indian contractor in Kansas and used his political and business connections well after the removal of these tribes from the state to aid the Missouri, Kansas & Texas railroad company, as its general manager, in laying the first track through the domain of the Five Civilized Tribes to the south.

Stevens first came to the attention of the Indian Office when, working as a partner in a Kansas Territory law firm, he contracted with the federal government to become agent for one of the early, more dramatic Indian land sales—that of the Confederated Kaskaskia, Peoria, Piankeshaw, and Wea Indians as provided in their 1854 treaty. The territorial governor, James Denver, warned Stevens that he should endeavor by "firmness and discretion" to overcome any "combinations or arrangements" entered into by speculators to obstruct fair sale of the land. Denver also advised that the sale must be held at Paola rather than Lecompton, where political and economic rings wishing to extend their influence to Indian lands were common. Stevens conducted the sale and thereby established connections not only with the local businessmen but with the ever-present, cooperative half-blood, in this case one Baptiste Peoria, who eventually, thanks to Stevens, was to control vast amounts of land in the region originally designated as Indian allotments. Peoria aided Stevens in the construction of a land office headquarters in record time and, despite rumors that the unsettled conditions of the territory would not allow for a sale to be held in safety, this one was conducted without a hitch. In June and July, 1857, Stevens sold 207,758 acres for $346,671. He collected nearly $10,000 for his part in the sale, the clerk and register got another $6,000, and $3,000 went to a local law firm which argued a taxation case against Kansas Territory on behalf of the tribe.[26]

In 1863 the Indians, who in this instance numbered only a few hundred, mounted a protest against the operation.

They said that Stevens always sold to a bidder for the lowest possible amount and that the money they gained from the sale was invested by the government in stocks and bonds without their consent. While Stevens sold most of the land at Paola as instructed by Denver, six parcels, by his own admission, did not sell. According to the Indian account, Stevens put some of these, amounting to 900 acres, on sale the next year at Lecompton and allowed only six men to bid on them, selling the bulk to J. B. Chapman, a railroad promoter and close acquaintance of Stevens'. Chapman failed to pay for the land, although the Indians had assumed he would, and the deed was quietly transferred to Stevens. The Indians also complained that they were forced by Stevens to sell another tract, over 5,000 acres of heavily timbered land, for $1.25 an acre, and that he got $1,000 from interested parties for accomplishing that. Nothing was done about the Indians' complaints.[27]

Meanwhile, Stevens established what was to be his real base in the Indian contracting business—the building of houses under contract from the Indian Office for the benefit of the Sac and Fox and Kansa tribes. The Kansa and the Sac and Fox treaties of 1859 provided that houses should be built for these tribes with the proceeds of land they were to cede. Stevens was granted the house-building concession for the Kansas immediately, and for the Sac and Fox in 1860, after the first contractor, Thomas McCage, had failed. Specifications for these buildings were outlined in the contracts negotiated by the Indian Office. The Sac and Fox houses, for instance, were to cost $180 and have dimensions of 16 x 18 feet. They were to have two doors and two windows, one floor of oak and an upper floor of walnut laid on stone supports, with a roof of walnut shingles. These specifications surely showed the abundance of good timber on the Indian reserves, and at first the tribes seemed well satisfied. The Sac and Fox agent, Perry Fuller, wrote in 1860 that those Indians without houses were jealous and might destroy the ones that were being built. He said that a larger contract should be negotiated so that status symbols could be distributed more widely.[28]

One of the difficulties that arose was as much the Indian Office's responsibility as it was Stevens'. Since the Indians and the government were both eager to get the houses built, and the land sales that were to finance the construction had not yet taken place, Stevens was paid for the houses in what was called Sac and Fox and Kansa scrip. This was a paper obligation issued by the Interior Department to pay the bearer out of the Indian trust funds when the lands were sold. There was no precise authority of law for this procedure, and it came back to haunt everyone when the Civil War interrupted the sale of Indian lands in Kansas and the scrip began to circulate on the open market. In 1861 Keokuk and others wrote to Sac and Fox agent C. C. Hutchinson that while the tribe was absent on a hunt the contract with Stevens for houses had been closed without their knowledge. The houses were constructed of green timber, they wrote, and were not in the places they wanted them. The same was true on the Kansa reserve. The poor construction, combined with Indian habits, meant that the red man often used the houses for stables or not at all, while they continued to live in their native dwellings. J. P. Usher, the secretary of the Interior, while in Kansas in 1862, inspected the work of Stevens and found it lacking. So did Indian commissioner Dole. The former advised that Stevens was not entitled to the sum he claimed, and that usually he demanded one-fourth to one-third more than the work was worth, as well as other "claims" for work not specified in the contracts. The "stairs" in the Kansa houses were nothing but step-ladders of joists with cleats nailed on them. Still Stevens was paid a great deal of his claim, partly because of his position as agent for the sale of bonds for the Kansas state government, which the Indian Office was buying from him as a way of investing Indian trust funds while at the same time aiding a frontier state. The houses brought Stevens a tidy profit of $109,000 on the Sac and Fox and $79,000 on the Kansa reserves. For the houses of six chiefs alone he asked

$15,700. Twenty years later, when Stevens became a member of Congress from New York, he persuaded that body to certify an appropriation to make up the difference of any reduction of his claims through the Indian Office action in the sixties. An Indian Territory newspaper, familiar with his activities there as a railroad man, commented: "It is believed in Kansas where the houses were built that Stevens got his pay at the time but that he, finally getting into Congress from New York, saw an opportunity and went forth. Our pale faced brothers seem not slow to learn the beauties of an appropriation." Stevens was a veritable Indian ring by himself, simultaneously assuming virtually all the roles. He had several opportunities to become an Indian agent himself but declined, probably because he realized there were more efficient means of getting ahead.[29]

The matter of the Stevens scrip is an indication of just how involved contracting could be and how far it could stray from serving Indian interests in the abstract. When the scrip remained unpaid after the Civil War, complaints poured into the Indian Office from all over the country, where hundreds of investors holding it had gained direct financial interest in the sale of Sac and Fox and Kansa lands. One investor, from Rochester, New York, agreed to relinquish 10 percent of the face value of the scrip in order to recover anything. "No government is so unrelenting as ours," he said, 'in demanding prompt payment of taxes . . . while an honest creditor of the government cannot even get a civil answer. At present it looks like swindling." The Interior Department could only reply that there were many demands upon the tribal funds, including those of the traders, and that these were paid in the order of presentation. Horatio Woodman, a Boston investor in scrip, charged that the whole affair convinced him that the Indian Office did business in a way unlike any other bureau of the government. He and others in a Bostonian investment group had $20,000 in Sac and Fox scrip, which they had purchased believing that the government was a responsible creditor. The holders of Stevens' scrip then added their voices to the outcry against the Indian ring, concluding that the Indian Office and Stevens must have been in collusion from the beginning to defraud innocent businessmen, under the guise of civilizing the Indians.[30]

For his part, Stevens bought a large amount of Sac and Fox land, over 52,000 acres valued at nearly $70,000, with scrip he held, thus converting a doubtful obligation into solid real estate. For example, on the New York Indian reserve he claimed to control at least 500 separate tracts. He managed to buy large amounts of land in the Delaware reserve through a corporation he formed to hold lands originally granted to Sarcoxie and other Delaware chiefs. As with most men operating with or through a ring, his ultimate reward was land in the new state of Kansas. The whole process meant that the members of the various Indian rings in the state became, with few exceptions, the intermediaries in the cultural revolution, both profiting thereby and ensuring that they would hold places of power in the new form of society that emerged from these difficulties.[31]

CHAPTER FOUR

The Government Chief

A VITAL FACTION necessary to the successful functioning of most Indian rings, it will be recalled, was tribal leadership. Without the helping hand of a chief or tribal council, speculators, congressmen, and government agents could look forward to material gain only under the most unusual circumstances. From the days of Washington and Jefferson to the end of the allotment revolution in the twentieth century, significant relationships between the white man and the Indians came down to a matter of legal maneuvers within the framework of treaties, statutes, and executive pronouncements orchestrated by the federal government. Such maneuvers generally required the signature of a tribal potentate, who, it was presumed, acted in the best interests of his people. That he often did not was a powerful device in the hands of an efficient Indian ring. In Kansas it was especially effective.

How were such Indian leaders identified? How were they persuaded to play the white man's game? Were their self-destructive actions the consequence of a congenital inability to perceive the invader's ultimate design? Was their alleged "noble savagery" simply too pervasive? Were their individual characters so weak that for a bottle of brandy, a handful of trinkets, and a modest plot of land they would relinquish the birthright of their people? Or were they victims of cultural erosion that with time became virtually irreversible?

What might be styled the traditional response to such questions has recently been offered by Vine Deloria, Jr., a Standing Rock Sioux and champion of contemporary Indian rights. Noting that the government was accustomed to treating with a king, queen, or other centralized authority, when it dealt with foreign powers, commissioners dealing with Indians insisted on negotiating with the supreme political leader of each tribe in their quest for valuable commodities. When no such individual could be found they created one— one who might best be described as the government chief. Finding the right person posed no real obstacle, according to Deloria. "The most pliable man who could be easily bribed was named chief and the treaty signed. Land cessions were often made and a tribe found itself on the way to a treeless desert before it knew what had happened."[1]

Applied to the coronation of certain government chiefs and their retinue in Kansas, there is something to be said for Deloria's analysis. A case in point is that reported by an angry delegation of Potawatomis in 1858. Forcefully expelled from their Indiana, Illinois, and Michigan Territory domain by the three treaties of 1832, and from Iowa Territory by the treaty of 1846, the traditionalist "Prairie" faction drew the line in 1858. They were completely satisfied with their well-timbered reservation on the Kansas River awarded in 1845. They were categorically opposed to allotments and the obliteration of communal land ownership. They were not uninformed regarding the land-grabbing tactics of Indian agent William E. Murphy and officials of the Leavenworth, Pawnee & Western Railroad, and they were especially distressed with the internal dissension created by a host of government chiefs. In an angry letter to the superintendent of Indian Affairs they reported that Murphy had advised them to sectionalize (i.e., accept allotments) or sell. But they wanted neither—not even when they were promised U.S.

citizenship as part of the deal. Citing solemn promises included in the Council Bluffs treaty of 1846, they stated:

> We are far enough west. Look over those treaties. Bear them in mind. Let them sink deep into your hearts, for they are sacred pledges and see what is our due, and your duty in them . . . . The Department has accused this nation of having no head. It is true. Who has caused it? Commissioners who acted under the seal of the United States. Within the space of twenty days on Tippecanoe River in 1832 you created twenty-eight chiefs by making Band Reserves in fee simple and we now have many aspiring men who make money their god. They sow the seeds of dissension.[2]

Ensuing events proved the veracity of these complaints, for by 1861 a treaty acceptable to the government, the L.P. & W., and the contrived Indian leadership had been concluded. As early as November, 1857, while admitting that the Potawatomis were being unduly pressured by half-bloods, mercenary whites, and "bad advisors" among their own ranks, Murphy nevertheless took the position that the Prairie Band, which comprised nearly one-third of the 3,500 total membership, was dragging its feet because of "their ignorant obstinacy." "Taken up with the dignity of their own race," complained a Leavenworth newspaper, "they declare they will be Indians as long as they live, that they will paint their faces and put as many rings in their noses as they please." They even boasted that they would "never pray, never work, and never send their children to school." To eliminate such deficiencies William Murphy determined to instruct the recalcitrants in the realities of progress. Emphasizing that those opposed to sectionalizing were virtually hemmed in by land-aggressive whites whose claims would unquestionably be recognized once Kansas achieved statehood, he advised them to allot, join with their Christian brethren, and thus preempt individual farmsteads before they were overrun by the white horde. But could not the Great White Father in

Washington prevent this? No, explained Murphy, even though he might wish to do so personally. The explanation —certainly not very convincing or comprehensible to the traditionalists—lay at the very foundation of the democratic system. To the accompaniment of not so veiled threats, he stated, "Let me impress upon your minds, my Red Children, that the white people who make the laws and elect the president and all other officeholders are the government themselves, and when they determine by a large majority to effect anything against the poor Indian, the president himself, though he might want to do right toward you, has not got the power to do it." As for himself, Murphy was quick to add that his only objective was justice for all concerned, and that in any case he had no personal interest in "speculation, town lots, etc."[3]

Under such circumstances the seeds of dissension sprouted rapidly and came to full bloom in the person of Anthony Navarre, an Indian of unconfirmed blood-quantum who was quick to gauge the power that went with being a government chief. With the self-proclaimed credentials of a "holy man" who only recently had been converted to Mormonism in the Kingdom of Deseret, Navarre made his appearance on the Potawatomi reserve just prior to the treaty of 1861. In short order he enjoyed a major following among the Prairie Band by preaching Mormonism and promising that when the Mormons had defeated the U.S. Army all Indian land would be returned to its original owners. He was opposed to sectionalizing, at least for the time being, and, according to Murphy, was the principal obstacle to the treaty sought by the government and railroad promoters. So impressed were the traditionalists with this "Wise man from the West" that they promised not to testify in the event he was brought before a white man's court of justice.[4]

A former student at Colonel Richard H. Johnson's Choctaw Academy in Kentucky—a training ground for other government chiefs as well—Navarre played his cards well. It required no divine insight to perceive that the Potawatomis were badly divided on the railroad-town development question and plagued with too many leaders. Nor was it difficult for a man of Navarre's principles and ambition to realize that the right credentials certified by the government at the right time might very well open the door to political power and personal gain. In short, he understood well how in concert with frontier economic interests and political charlatans of various persuasions the government used bribery as a tool in detribalization and Indian removal.[5]

As an increasingly prominent headman of the Prairie Band Navarre refused to sign the treaty of 1861 (even though he had no personal quarrel with its terms). In fact he played a prominent role in a subsequent protest signed by forty angry Potawatomis described by Agent Ross "as the wildest of fellows." Navarre's stature with the dissenters was thereby enhanced, so much so that they raised no objection to his accepting in fee simple a 160-acre plot from the government in recognition of his regal stature. Drafted by James C. Stone, president and major stockholder of the L.P. & W., and Thomas Ewing, Jr., first chief justice of the Kansas Supreme Court and prominent land jobber, the treaty of 1861 was designed to destroy tribal cohesion and satisfy the land and timber requirements of the L.P. & W. as it looked forward to government subsidies under the Pacific Railroad Act of 1862. As a sop to the Navarre dissenters, Article Four provided for a diminished reserve to be held in common by the noncitizen group. Understandably, this created confusion and concern, particularly after 1862 when the railroad crowd learned that the Citizen Potawatomis were selecting the best-timbered lands along the projected right of way, and that the only realistic solution might be to move the entire tribe south to Indian country. Rumors to this effect prompted many of the allotted Potawatomis to flock back to the diminished reserve with high hopes they might be compensated if it were placed on the auction block. The situation played into the hands of Navarre, and other opportunists whose power and prestige in the eyes of the government were increasing.[6]

To avert the impending crisis, the Indian Office in Washington paid heed to the advice of Ross. He was on the scene, had participated in the Free-Soil Convention in Topeka in 1857, had been a delegate to the Republican National Convention in 1860, had a clear understanding of the political climate, and had worked with the railroad clique from the start. Indeed, he had been virtually hand-picked as the Potawatomi agent by the L.P. & W. crowd in 1861. In order to facilitate the normal transaction of business that was suffering from "incredible divisions," advised Ross, it was mandatory that the foundation of Potawatomi leadership be taken from the traditional chiefs and headmen and given to a more efficient "business committee" comprised of notables representing both factions. For the Citizen Band he recommended John Tipton and Louis View, and for the Prairie Band, M. B. Beaubien, J. N. Bourassa, and A. F. Navarre. In the final determination Tipton's name was withdrawn in favor of B. N. Bertrand, a close confidant of the L.P. & W. leadership and principal tribal promoter of the St. Marys town site, where, according to Agent Luther Palmer, "the whole community are more or less interested in having a general business and shipping point established." It was chief-making at its best, and by the flick of a pen the government had certified a conniving cadre of Potwatomi leaders without a word of warning or explanation to the rank and file. View, Beaubien, Bertrand, and Bourassa had demonstrated their loyalty by signing the treaty of 1861. But because Navarre had not, he took the position of one entitled to even greater deference and reward for playing ball with the government and the railroad crowd.[7]

As it turned out, Navarre was a novice functionary in the emerging Potawatomi ring, which is not to say that he was ignored for attempting to keep the Prairie Band in line. At his insistence Ross demanded that the business committee be paid at least $200 a year because "they worked so hard." No money whatsoever was to be given to the now inconsequential traditional "chiefs." Since Navarre had received a miserly 160 acres as a lowly headman, he now was entitled to twice that amount in recognition of his greater responsibilities on the committee. On neither score did the Indian Office object. And during the critical months of 1868, when Senator Samuel C. Pomery of Kansas and promoters of the Atchison, Topeka, & Santa Fe railroad were gaining a foothold on the Potawatomi lands where the Union Pacific, Eastern Division railroad (successor to the L.P. & W.) had left in frustration, Navarre shared with Bourassa and Bertrand a $6,000 trip to Washington to firm up the details of one of the more notorious land steals concluded in Kansas. Their expense money came from tribal coffers at the insistence of Navarre, Bourassa, and Bertrand, who covered their tracks by refusing to deal with the Indian Office unless it declined to fund a similar trip to Washington by certain malcontents of the Prairie Band. As Luther Palmer put it to Superintendent Thomas Murphy, "I fear that the great desire of many persons to be prominent and to go to Washington will lead them to forget that Indian Tribes are dependent rather than independent sovereignties, and wards instead of greatly needed allies of the government of the United States."[8]

Navarre played along with his associates on the business committee. He lobbied for and eventually signed the amendatory treaty of 1866, which granted quarter sections of land to all adult Potawatomis, regardless of sex or family headship. Since he stood to gain personally, self-interest, of course, played a large role in his actions. More important, however, was pressure exerted by Bourassa, a Potawatomi by marital connection, who complained to Palmer that in 1861 he and his family had been promised no less than 800 acres by the then ruling "chiefs." Bourassa admitted he should have advanced his claim at the time, but because of pressing "business affairs" in Missouri and the disruptive situation in Kansas during the Civil War, he had been unable to do so. Now, in 1867, he had presented the matter to the business committee, who were pleased to recommend him for "a favorable consideration." Bourassa's tactics obviously were nefarious, but fully in line with business committee procedure and, more importantly, Ross's strategy. As early as March, 1863, Ross had advised the Indian Office on the best policy to be pursued with regard to white men (like Bourassa) who had married Potawatomi women:

> It would be simple justice that now when the major portion of the Potawatomies are about to cast off forever the last relic of barbarism and take their position in the world as civilized people that these men who at an early day married the daughters of the tribe through the best of motives and who have been the means of accomplishing this much desired result, should be equal participants in the division of the soil.[9]

Soon after the Bourassa accommodation Navarre's influence on the committee and with the Prairie Band began to deteriorate. In large measure this was a consequence of the A.T. & S.F. land deal negotiated in Washington in February, 1867, and proclaimed eighteen months later. When word of its proposed stipulations reached Kansas several spokesmen who identified themselves as traditional Potawatomi chiefs journeyed to Atchison where they complained to Thomas Murphy that the business committee was grossly mishandling tribal affairs. Perhaps not then fully cognizant of the unfolding scandal, Murphy turned a deaf ear and wrote to Commissioner Nathan G. Taylor in Washington, "I regard them [the business committee] as among the most intelligent men of the nation and believe them incapable of knowingly transacting any business that would result in detriment to their people." At that time the treaty had not yet been enacted, and in fairness it should be noted that Navarre did not affix his signature to the final document. Bertrand, Beaubien, and Bourassa did, as did Murphy and Palmer. Bourassa enjoyed the additional honor of serving as the official United States interpreter, for which he doubtless received additional compensation. A more severe indictment came on October 23, 1868, and again on March 11, 1870, when Alexander Bushman, an Indiana Potawatomi who had been informed that all naturalized Potawatomis would receive money under the treaty, wrote Taylor that he had journeyed to Kansas to claim his share, only to find that it was not that simple. Indeed, it was very expensive. Armed with a power of attorney conferred by "a great number of half-breeds," the business committee demanded that for each individual payment they were empowered to take 12 percent, which came to an average of $75 for each member on the tribal roll. Worse, former agents Ross and Palmer (Palmer was replaced by Joel Morris in the Grant administrative shuffle of 1869) were in on the deal from the start, and with the business committee they expected to collect the grand sum of $45,000 for their efforts. "It is ridiculous for them to rape the poor Indians," complained Bushman, "and I hope you will be merciful to the ignorant and instruct their agent to do away with the committee."[10]

This was not the case, for a "general tribal council" that elected one head chief, two secondary chiefs, four advisory braves, and a new business committee, comprised of George Young, Bourassa, E. G. Nadeau, and Navarre, was, in December, 1869, routinely certified by the Indian Office without a word of protest. It was leadership bordering on anarchy, yet wholly acceptable to the Potawatomi ring. On the other hand, it carried with it the seeds of its own destruction. Once the consequences of the 1867 treaty became apparent, factions cutting across band lines began to coalesce around a common cause. They complained that the business committee had in fact sold out to the A.T. & S.F. speculators for money that was distributed to only a select few. Suspicious eyes were cast on Young and Bourassa of the Citizen Band, but it was Navarre who received the brunt of criticism. Try as he would this confused government lackey was unable to convince his followers that he was a man of honest purpose, nor was he able to prevent his fellow councilmen from casting him in the role of scapegoat. They had signed the treaty, he had not. In the end, however, it made little difference.[11]

A glaring example of fraud by the Potawatomi leadership is seen in the machinations of Alexander Rushmore, who married a Shawnee girl to secure a financial subsidy from the government and who then determined to "sectionalize with the Potawatomis" for the purpose of increasing his personal wealth. By any reasonable appraisal it was a brazen act, but not unrealistic in terms of the government's conduct of Indian affairs in Kansas. Fearful, no doubt, that their own chicanery might become public knowledge, the business committee refused to enroll Rushmore for an easy handout. The frustrated Shawnee pretender then retaliated by journeying to Washington armed with documents sympathetic to his cause. These documents purported to demonstrate that he had secured the power of tribal attorney through the cooperation of "certain parties in Washington working in concert with the Potawatomi leadership on the frontier," and that he was to receive no less than 30 percent on the collection of all claims he personally processed through the right channels under the treaty of 1867. Not fully informed about all aspects of the situation, Agent Morris sent an angry letter to Superintendent Hoag, stating that Rushmore, though unsuccessful in this instance, obviously was one of those men who worked largely for their own advantage. Whether it was Navarre, or Bourassa, or the entire business committee who had specifically encouraged the likes of Rushmore made little difference. A watershed in Potawatomi history had been reached—the local leadership was bypassed and an appeal made directly to Washington. Fearful of similar frauds on all sides, the tribal majority took the advice of the Indian Office and demanded Navarre's resignation for failing to exercise proper leadership. Writing to Hoag, Morris reported that the Prairie Band's confidence in *any* leadership was so badly shaken that they had categorically refused to allow the annual annuity census to be taken, which in turn was preventing the issuance of land patents to the Citizen Band and, more importantly, to the railroad. It was an impossible, totally unacceptable situation, warned Morris, and the whole matter came down to bad leadership, "especially that of A. T. Navarre who drinks heavily and who probably did so at the time of the 1867 treaty." Nothing was said about Navarre's opposition to the treaty in question, nor was anything said about the performance of Bertrand, Beaubien, and Bourassa, let alone that of Ross, Palmer, and the A.T. & S.F. And, of course, nothing was said about the government's abortive promotion of Navarre as a Potawatomi chief. In the end he had failed to perform as expected and was cast aside as so much excess baggage.[12]

Applied to the Potawatomi leadership debacle, Deloria's analysis is essentially correct. Traditionally, the various villages came under the jurisdiction of three blood-chiefs who enjoyed their positions by inheritance and the display of sound judgment. Until disrupted by the government in Kansas these chiefs enjoyed profound authority in the administration of civil and criminal matters. Only in times of war with other tribes was this tripartite leadership obliged to defer to councilors and possibly other dissidents in the Potawatomi community. In Kansas, however, where land in fee simple was essential to railroad and town development, tradition meant nothing. Ironically, the invader had not the good sense to realize that the Prairie Band had in fact played a secondary role in tribal affairs for years, and thus was an illogical faction to manipulate with an unreliable government chief. In large measure this explains why the demise of Navarre was accompanied by little fanfare, whether from the tribe or the government.[13]

While the Citizen Band prevailed and eventually lost many of their allotments to squatters and nearly 200,000 acres at an average of a dollar an acre to such railroad magnates as Willis Gaylord, Thomas Ewing, Jr., William Borland, and Sidney Clarke, the practice of chief-making continued at a brisk pace elsewhere. As early as 1854, by the Shawnee allotment treaty concluded in Washington by George Manypenny, Chiefs Joseph Parks and Black Hoof had received nearly 2,000 extra acres of land for cooperating to the fullest extent with the government. Article Two of the treaty was especially controversial in that it allowed the privilege of selecting allotments to "every head of a family, who, although not a Shawnee, may have been legally married to a Shawnee, according to the customs of that people." Since the Shawnee domain was perhaps the most strategically located reserve in all of the Kansas Territory—situated, as it was, immediately west of Missouri and south of the Kansas River—town-site speculators and land jobbers of various sorts appeared in droves.[14]

Leading the pack was Paschal Fish, a half-blood Shawnee who in the words of his attorney was "an educated person of exceedingly shrewd instinct." Even in a land of crooks and contrasts, this was no exaggeration. In 1857 Fish entered into a contract with a company of Germans in Chicago for the sum of $5,000, which gave them title to half the town lots on a proposed 800-acre tract southwest of the Shawnee Mission. Immediate construction plans called for seventy-five houses, a large sawmill, a grist mill, a shingle mill, graded streets, and a bridge over Nakanwa Creek—an enterprise conservatively valued at $100,000. The problem was that sending every deed to Washington for congressional or executive approval was a stumbling block to progress. Indeed, charged Edward Clark, the only important result was that many Shawnees would be "unduly injured." Fish had contacted James Denver, who had advised that if Congress did not act as required by the 1854 treaty he would have the right to issue the patents. But since Fish was not absolutely certain and, in any case, was wholly frustrated by all the bureaucracy, would not the secretary rule on the situation with dispatch? Others were experiencing similar difficulties, including those promoting the towns of Tecumseh, De Soto, Chillicothe, and Shawnee City.[15]

Probably because of the impending election of 1860 and the tenuous position of most Buchanan appointees, no executive directives were immediately forthcoming. Like so many other bureaucrats in Kansas, Shawnee agent B. J. Newsom was cast upon his own resources. From nearby Missouri, pro-slave squatters came by the hundreds and were especially attracted to the communally held Black Bob reserve, a strategically located 33,392-acre tract guaranteed to the followers of Shawnee Black Bob who in 1854 had refused to accept allotment in severalty and who thereby encouraged an intratribal struggle for power that had been seething for several years. Traditionally, the Shawnees had been governed by three hereditary chiefs representing the three principal bands. The headmen in turn designated a principal leader, whose judgment and stature were never seriously challenged until the early fifties. John Francis inherited the exalted position upon the death of Chief Lauloway in 1850, and it was during his chieftainship that the young men of the tribe made their bid for power. Under government pressure accompanying the treaty of 1854 the pendulum of power finally swung in the opposite direction and "Captain" Joseph Parks was elected to head the Shawnees. He and those who succeeded him for the next decade and a half were the principal signatories of the treaty and, in effect, the first of the Shawnee government chiefs. Their principal opponent was Black Bob, who refused to accept the new dispensation and who continued to view himself as a traditional headman. Newsom was literally swamped with requests for the land patents which the profit-minded Shawnee allottees were only too eager to convey to the squatters.[16]

While there is some reason to believe that Newsom engaged in personal profiteering in the disposal of these patents, there is much more evidence about the role the chiefs played in the determination of official policy. For one thing, the treaty required that the allotments be surveyed before conveyance to white squatters; for another, in situations when a fair price could not be agreed upon, a final determination was to be made by the Shawnee leadership with the consent of the United States agent for that tribe. It is exceedingly doubtful if Newsom was formally advised of either requirement. Pressured on all sides to the extent that he could do little more than "fold the patents and arrange them in packages to be found as needed," he desperately requested further instructions from Washington. People who had already purchased their land hounded him day and night to determine what procedures were necessary to perfect their titles. Fish's attorney scoffed at Newsom's caution, chided him for submitting excessively high expense vouchers and complaining to Washington about having to work seven days a week, offered to handle all the transactions himself, and even boasted that he and others were sending representatives to Washington to complain of Newsom's gross inefficiency. The greatest pressure, however, came from the Shawnee leadership. Writing to Superintendent C. M. Robinson, Newsom reported that the chiefs were offended greatly by his cautious actions and demanded that he simply issue all patents upon request. This he apparently did, since, in his own words, "they were not the least interested in a fair price."[17]

Newsom's successor, James B. Abbott, was less cautious and certainly better informed regarding the government policy of having the right Indian leadership at the right place and time. Because many of the hastily drawn Newsom patents had to be invalidated by the secretary of the Interior in actions that led to litigation over tax assessments and creditors' claims lasting to the end of the century, it was mandatory that in the meanwhile the government manipulate the Shawnee leadership almost at will. Subtle methods, of course, were attempted, with bribery leading the list. But when these brought no results more arbitrary tactics were deployed, as was the case when Joseph Parks came up for reelection in 1862. The incident was reported by Abelard Guthrie, who, it will be recalled, was a man of not much greater principle than Navarre, Bourassa, or Parks.

The problem was that Guthrie harbored a grudge against the Shawnees because he and his wife, formerly of the Wyandot tribe, had been rejected for a Shawnee allotment. Guthrie charged that the rejection was because of his abolitionist leanings and his open criticism of the Methodist Episcopal Church, South—surely an oversimplification. In any case, with an eye for political preferment in Washington and a desire for personal gain, Guthrie kept a close eye on Black Bob's opposition to any further severalty

The End of Indian Kansas

treaties and on the Shawnee leadership in particular. When, in late 1865, it became apparent that the Black Bob reserve was in danger of being partitioned, Guthrie sent an angry letter to Washington in which he recalled the "election" of Chief Parks in 1862. Following an official announcement of the biannual election by Abbott, Black Bob and his followers had appeared at the designated time and cast ninety-four votes against Parks. Notably absent were the alloted Shawnees who met after sundown and cast sixty votes for Parks. The proceeding, of course, was boycotted by the Black Bobs. Apparently responding to instructions from on high, Abbott immediately repudiated the daytime election and recognized Parks and his slate as the duly elected council. Parks was reelected in 1864 and was then succeeded by Graham Rogers, Charles Bluejacket, and Charles Tucker—all acceptable to the government. None of the elections after the 1862 fiasco were attended by the Black Bobs, whose disillusionment was complete and was exceeded, perhaps, only by that of Guthrie. In a pamphlet which he published in 1868, at a time when one of the many efforts were made to bring the Black Bobs in line with government policy, the frustrated mixed-blood who claimed the Shawnees owed him $15,000 charged:

> For the last seven or eight years there have been the most persistent efforts on the part of Indian agents and speculators to get hold of Black Bob's and the absentee reserves, and six treaties have been made for that purpose. Five of them have been defeated, and it is to be hoped the sixth will share the same fate. Black Bob's people had nothing to do with making these treaties and yet they are the only parties who have lands to dispose of—who have any real interest in making a treaty at all. . . . While the Indians hold their lands in common they feel they are safe, and this feeling prompted them to prefer lands less valuable, where they could have them in a compact body. And the experience of the severalty Shawnees fully vindicates the wisdom of

their choice; for of those who received patents for their lands it is estimated that about one-half are now landless.[18]

On occasion some government officials found themselves in a situation so untenable that it was simply impossible to deny the more intricate details of chief-making. The stormy course encountered by promoters of the Atchison & Pike's Peak railroad in the assault on the Kickapoo reservation, it will be recalled, is one such example. Although eventually implemented in spite of widespread protest from potential white settlers as well as most of the Kickapoos themselves, the brazen tactics involved in the allotment treaty of 1862 prompted the Indian commissioner, William Dole, to send special investigators to Kansas to demand a grand jury investigation in Topeka. Charges and countercharges flew freely, but in the final analysis the contending railroad interests pulling at cross purposes neutralized the investigation and shielded Kickapoo agent Charles Keith and Senator Samuel Pomeroy from any convictable crime. However, during the course of the investigation Keith stated that it was the government's practice to keep the Indians in a state of subordination, and that no agent could execute this responsibility unless he had the power and ability to unseat traditional chiefs who were uncooperative. Taken in conjunction with reports from Kansas citizens in 1863 that of the eight Kickapoos who signed the treaty one was the tribal interpreter, another a woman, and still another a ten-year-old boy, Keith's testimony was classic evidence of Indian leadership manipulation. For his efforts, which by no means were exclusive, this successful chief-maker obtained two sections of Kickapoo land by transfer from the A. & P.P. to his wife and $7,000 from a 1,330-acre plot he sold to Pomeroy shortly after the treaty had been implemented.[19]

The making of paper chiefs among the Kickapoos did not end with the departure of Keith. He was replaced by Abram Bennett in May, 1864, and then by Franklin G. Adams in March, 1865. In the meantime it was assumed that the Kickapoos would rush forward to take their allotments, but the outrageous circumstances accompanying the treaty worked against this; try as the government would, very few individuals offered to stake their claims. So infuriated was Nokowhat that he departed southward with 100 members of his band, while Keoquark went to western Kansas in company with 50 of his followers. Of the 265 who remained in northeastern Kansas, by 1869 only 93 had accepted their allotments. Those who retained their lands in common leveled charges of fraud against Washington in general and Adams in particular for his impatient demands that the allotment revolution proceed on schedule. This was too much for Thomas Murphy, in nearby Atchison, who had not been party to the original negotiations and who in classical bureaucratic style took the path of least resistance by blaming the Kickapoo leadership for their unfortunate state of affairs. Depicting Adams as a responsible public servant and unwilling scapegoat, Murphy charged that four of the Kickapoos who had signed the treaty—Par-thee, Ke-aw-guak, Pet-ti-quauk, and Ken-ne-kuk—were not leaders at all. Because Keith had erred seriously in 1862 when he had accepted their signatures, the time had come to alter the situation for the better.

> They are not fit to be chiefs [insisted Murphy], and they live remotely from the rest of the tribe and never meet with them to consult or advise. They not only get drunk and gamble themselves but encourage others to do so as well. They are against schools, churches and agricultural progress, and are selfish, caring nothing for their people. They refuse to transact any allotment business with their agent, and we should remove them as quickly as possible. I recommend new men who are traditional chiefs, Mes-que-qua, Ke-o-tuk, and Os-aw-wa.[20]

It was a recommendation insulting in the extreme and patently indicative of government duplicity, for by 1866 it mattered not in the least who the recognized tribal leaders were. Directors and lobbyists for the A. & P.P. were in firm control of the situation and fully protected by Article Ten of the 1862 treaty, which provided that unless the absentee Kickapoos returned within one year of the date the treaty was ratified, they would, excluding a miserly 40-acre tract to be occupied and cultivated according to government specifications, forfeit all rights to the land. In addition, "in every respect they were to be governed by the same rules and regulations as is prescribed for the government of the lands reserved by the preceding articles." If they refused, as was generally the case, their lands were to be sold to settlers for the benefit of those alloted Kickapoos who had remained on the original reserve. It was an open-and-shut case, and no more fitting tribute to the government's calculated design to destroy the Kickapoo leadership can be identified than the decision of Pet-ti-quauk, who in December, 1865, conveyed his allotment in full to Samuel Pomeroy.[21]

As reserve after reserve went under the hammer, Indian agents and tribal dignitaries alike were expected to perform as mere puppets in the hands of powerful, corporate interests. Reeling under the immense power of the L.P. & W., Delaware chief John Conner finally conceded in 1862 that his people had too many counselors and that the number should be reduced so that "the few best men" might better deal with allotment and removal to the area south of Kansas with greater efficiency. Four years later, during a particularly critical stage in the Osage treaty of 1865 that ceded over four million acres of land to the government, Osage agent George C. Snow reported that "he knew all about this chief matter." A faction of young Osages objected to an amendment to the treaty that provided lucrative considerations for the Leavenworth, Lawrence & Galveston railroad and the Union Pacific, Southern Branch (Katy). The faction was led by Joseph Paw-ne-no-pos-he, a full-blood who had been educated at the mission school, who could read and write, and who was determined to unseat those Osage leaders who had agreed to the amendment. In an angry and extremely candid letter to Washington Snow complained:

All the old chiefs are bitterly opposed to Paw-ne-no-pos-he. White Hair is the legal chief of the nation and it would not do for an agent to appoint a chief contrary to their custom. This letter by Paw-ne-no-pos-he was gotten up in my presence as an appeal from my decision to the President of the United States last September when I called a council to get the amendment to their treaty signed. I would have arrested Paw-ne-no-pos-he and Wa-to-in-ka and put them in confinement instead of buying them up two or three times, if I had the military force. I believe the government will have to intervene in this matter and put down this faction so the chiefs can rule their people. As it is they have but very little influence over their young men.[22]

Snow was eventually forced to flee to Little Rock, Arkansas, to escape the violent threats of the nontreaty faction, and for this he deserves some sympathy. Yet his insistence that it was not general government policy to tamper with tribal leadership was at best deceiving and at worst a deliberate fraud. In fact, Snow knew better. Like public functionaries in comparable circumstances, he obviously was administering the Osage agency in conformity with a policy most white people understood only too well, but which few had the courage to discuss in an open forum.[23]

The sheer quantity of like incidents warrants the conclusion that in the two decades after 1854 the emigrant tribes in eastern Kansas were virtually run by government-sponsored (and selected) chiefs. In 1863, for example, a group of New York chiefs who had been bought off found it impossible to revoke their self-imposed power of attorney when they realized that the consequences were as detrimental to themselves as to the people they presumably represented. In 1862 Chief Sarcoxie of the Delawares was placed on the federal payroll with the full understanding that he would cooperate regardless of the circumstances. However, the liabilities of such an agreement prompted the crafty leader to shock the Indian Office into disbelief when, in 1864, he demanded, with no success, an insurance policy for his high risk position. Of the five government chiefs who signed the critically significant Miami land-cession treaty of 1854, two were a father and son team, "drunken, sottish, degraded, ignorant, and with neither in possession of even one-fourth Miami blood." And for what surely must stand as the classic example of tribal manipulation, one need only examine the incredible career of John Tauy (Tecumseh) Jones, who, in league with Ottawa agent Clinton C. Hutchinson and Baptist divine I. S. Kalloch, pampered, cajoled, cheated, and finally dominated Ottawa chiefs John Wilson, William Hurr, and James Wind over control of the Ottawa Indian University.[24]

The tenuous political power of men like Navarre, Black Bob, Ken-ne-kuk, Sarcoxie, and Wilson *vis-à-vis* their many tribal and nontribal detractors suggests that Indian leadership was never very competent in Kansas and that outside interests, whether public or private or both, could manage matters almost at will. Like so many bungling buffoons, they were cynical, shortsighted, and easily isolated into factions, with the result that in tribal dissolution and removal they must be charged with major responsibility on grounds that more principled and mature native leaders might have been able to ward off the invader. But such analysis overestimates the white impact on Indian political leadership and fails to recognize that many tribes were plagued with factionalism long before they were removed from Kansas. P. Richard Metcalf has recently argued that by focusing simultaneously on indigenous Indian leadership problems of long standing and on subsequent white cultural inroads, the historian for the first time may obtain a more realistic picture of Indian political behavior and thus bridge the gap between white-oriented and Indian-oriented history. In a particularly significant passage Metcalf states that too much attention to white causality and white-related issues has made all postcontact Indian political activity appear to have been directed at dealing with the white problem. Yet there was a period of transition between first white contact and total orientation to white-provoked issues, during which time indigenous problems and issues continued to be primary determinants of Indian political behavior and the white presence was a minor issue. The length of this period generally depended on how long it took for the white presence to become overwhelming, but many ancient divisions and political antagonisms were extremely durable.[25]

An example of such durability and transition is that of the Kansa-Kaws who were subjected to as much outside pressure in the period after 1854 as any other tribe in Kansas. According to Étienne Veniard de Bourgmont, who visited them in the middle Missouri valley in 1724 near the future site of Kansas City, the Kansa-Kaws recognized no less than seven village chiefs and twelve war chiefs who did not always see eye to eye on important matters of state. Nearly a century later, in 1811, Fort Osage factor George C. Sibley reported that the war councils were "much distracted by jealousies arising from the ambition and turbulent disposition of some of the warriors and minor chiefs." Whereas Bourgmont's report dated back to a time when there had been little if any previous white contact, Sibley's information clearly reflected the squabbles attendant to the highly competitive fur trade conducted by French-Catholic merchants operating out of St. Louis. Within the next few years an outsider appeared on the scene. His appearance, for all practical purposes, inaugurated the period when white influences became overwhelming. He was White Plume, son of the great Osage chief Pawhuska, who as a result of inter- and intratribal factionalism and a good deal of personal ambition, was recognized by the United States as the principal Kansa-Kaw chief in 1825. In that year, in St. Louis, White Plume readily agreed to a major land cession that provided 640-acre allotments to twenty-three half-bloods, four of whom were his own grandchildren. Two years later, when it became apparent that the followers of Fool Chief, Hard Chief, and American Chief would have nothing to do with White Plume and his Catholic half-bloods, the government chief complained bitterly of factionalism and the danger of having too many chiefs. To reinstate cordial relations he insisted that the government build him a substantial stone house near agency headquarters and provide a priest to minister to himself and his people. This was done, but with ill consequences for the welfare of his people.[26]

Following a second land-cession treaty in 1846 and the opening of Kansas Territory in 1854, the 250,000-acre Kansa-Kaw reservation near Council Grove was overrun by squatters, land jobbers, and railroad promoters with finesse, and in the years following the Civil War it became evident that the tribe would be forced to leave Kansas. By the time they made their final trek to future Kay County, Oklahoma, in 1873, the Kansa-Kaws were so divided in matters political that the Rock Creek, Kahola, Picayune, and Half-Blood bands were conducting themselves as separate tribelets. Yet the Half-Bloods, with a good deal of government assistance, managed to dominate business affairs in the closing years of the nineteenth century, and when the Kansa-Kaws were allotted in 1902 the heirs of White Plume enjoyed a comfortable majority.[27]

Similar difficulties plagued the Potawatomis and Osages, but in terms of impact on ultimate tribal disintegration the Sac and Fox leadership crisis in Kansas is without rival. Like the Uncas-Sasscus feud among the Mohegan-Pequots in early seventeenth-century New England, or the stormy political career of Pushmataha of the Choctaws nearly two centuries later, the struggle between Black Hawk and Keokuk for political power in the period following the War of 1812 displays a flaw in Sac and Fox politics that worsened in the 1850s, after the tribe had been forced to take up residence in Kansas.[28]

Black Hawk's prestige was based on his accomplishments in the field of battle, his respect for ancient Sac traditions, his anti-American diplomacy, and his stubborn refusal to sign away valuable tribal lands east of the Mississippi. Keokuk, on the other hand, signed four major treaties with the United States (including the 1842 document that forced the Sacs and Foxes to remove from Iowa to Kansas). He also was a master at standing in the background, playing faction against faction to his own political advantage. When peace was restored following the Black Hawk War of 1832 the United States recognized Keokuk as the principal chief, while Black Hawk was relegated to a minor position. Black Hawk died in 1837, in relative obscurity; Keokuk died in 1848, at which time the chieftaincy passed on to his son Moses—also known as Keokuk. As expected, the younger Keokuk attempted to continue his father's style of governance, but by the mid-1850s this was becoming increasingly difficult. For one thing, many of his followers were convinced that the move from Iowa to Kansas had been a tragic mistake. Their lands on the upper Marais des Cygnes River were inferior, and they were being victimized by whiskey peddlers, land sharks, and irresponsible government agents. Moreover, a faction known as the "Missouri Sacs and Foxes" steadfastly refused to inhabit a small reserve in northern Kansas that had been provided by the extremely questionable treaty of 1854.[29]

The principal leaders who fought the government plan to collect all Sacs and Foxes in Kansas and then in future Oklahoma were Pow-a-shick and Ne-sour-quoit (sometimes spelled Ne-son-quoit) of the Missouri faction, and Mut-tut-tah and Mo-ko-ho-ko of Keokuk's group. Unlike Pow-a-shick, who simply refused to have anything to do with the 1854 deliberations and who thereby was cast aside much like Black Hawk had been in the 1830s, Ne-sour-quoit apparently was duped into signing without fully comprehending how the treaty would break up the communal land base of his people. The more he complained, however, the more rigid Agent Daniel Vanderslice became. When, in 1857, Ne-sour-quoit's reputation among his followers was enhanced by his refusal to attend the government annuity distribution and "to take over his own field," Vanderslice's patience was exhausted. Describing his detractor as opposed to farming, education, Christianity, civilization, and "without a doubt the most refractory chief" in the entire Indian country, Vanderslice reported to Washington that he had dismissed Ne-sour-quoit as an official Sac and Fox chief. Infuriated, the aging leader traveled to Washington at his own expense to present his case directly to Acting Commissioner Charles Mix. By the time he arrived in Washington in late December, 1857, however, a letter from Pe-to-oke-o-mah and twelve of the so-called "progressive" faction in Kansas was on file in the Indian Office, in which it was charged that Ne-sour-quoit's complaints were nothing more than a deception to cover up secret dealings with certain white men of bad reputation, other bad Indians, and an obscure character known only as "Mexican George." While these charges were not immediately confirmed or rejected, Ne-sour-quoit's complaint that he had never seen the final draft of the treaty of 1854 fell on deaf ears, and Mix took the occasion to scold the Sac and Fox leader for his childlike behavior. Prefacing his remarks with the statement that the Great Father dreamed at night how he might best protect and benefit his red children, Mix continued:

> The children of your white brethren acquire parents to guide them and advise them, because the sense which the great spirit puts into the head of children doesn't expand or mature until they grow to be men; but Ne-sour-quoit and your party don't appear to be growing from children to manhood like the whites, but appear to be children all the time. Hence it is that your great father sends his white brethren out to protect and advise you, and if needs be, chastise you for your obstinancy.

More than a year later, when it was determined that Ne-sour-quoit's trip to Washington had apparently been financed by timber speculators in the pay of future Kansas governor Thomas Carney, the disillusioned Sac and Fox traditionalist gave up his fight and "joined up with the other chiefs."[30]

On the Marais des Cygnes reserve Keokuk was faced with no lack of ambitious would-be chiefs, whose connections were well secured with government agents or private speculators, or both. As pressure mounted for full-scale allotment and/or complete removal to future Oklahoma, it was patently clear that no one leader could hold all the factions together.

While a local paper smugly described the Sacs and Foxes as "fast fellows who squander their annuities within a few days," Keokuk demanded that the government write down all official talks so there would be "no more maybes" regarding future treaty stipulations. It was, however, a futile effort, as Keokuk himself probably knew. Ka-sha-mah-me, who was appointed chief by Francis Tymany for no better reason than to sign the treaty of 1859, was fired a few months later by Perry Fuller for "drinking and other bad habits." In the mid-sixties an Irishman named Henry Donahoe, who had married a Sac and Fox woman, was recognized as the principal chief. But this report runs contrary to another which stated that the tribe was in fact wholly "in the hands of four drunken rowdies"—including, no doubt, George Powers, who ran a public house at Centrapolis, fifteen miles from agency headquarters, and Joseph Goky, both of whom made certain that in the treaty of 1867 they were awarded substantial allotments in fee simple. In the final analysis, it was Mo-ko-ho-ko who made the last challenge against Keokuk and the government.[31]

To Keokuk, Mo-ko-ho-ko was what Black Hawk had been to the former's father. Stubbornly traditional and wholly committed to holding the Sacs and Foxes together by the retention of a common land base, he was tragically undone by one of his close followers, Mut-tut-tah, who signed the removal treaty of 1867 while Mo-ko-ho-ko was absent from the reservation nursing an injury sustained on a hunting trip to the Arkansas valley. Certainly, there is every reason to believe that Mut-tut-tah was bought off, for upon his return Mo-ko-ho-ko charged fraud and collusion with Agent Henry Martin. Perhaps it did not really matter, for by then the government could easily have engaged the services of some other "chief" in Mo-ko-ho-ko's band. As squatters broke down fences and rushed to secure the best Sac and Fox lands fully two years before the actual removal took place in December, 1869, even Keokuk had second thoughts about the unfolding debacle. He refused to allow a delegation to travel south to search out new lands, whereupon the government quickly appointed Ne-graw-ho in his place, with the explanation that "unless Keokuk is given a setback by the Dept. he will ride rough-shod over his agent and everyone else, paying no attention to the wishes or instructions of government officials."[32]

In a fitting climax to nearly two decades of government chief-making in Kansas, Mo-ko-ho-ko and about two hundred of his followers refused to journey south to the new Canaan. Some returned to Iowa, others joined with the few remnant Sacs in southern Nebraska, while still others took up temporary residence with the Prairie Potawatomis in Kansas. Repeatedly faced with sickness and starvation, they were forcibly removed to Indian Territory in 1876, but within a short time they returned to the Marais des Cygnes valley in Kansas, which they still considered to be their own. Here and there they occupied small plots considered undesirable by the speculators, but for the most part they hired themselves out as day laborers to the white farmers who had ousted them a decade earlier.[33]

CHAPTER FIVE

The Claim of the Soil

IN ORDER TO TRANSFORM NATURE fully, it was of course necessary not only to cross the land but to possess it. The inroads of corporate directors, federal officials, and government chiefs would be lent permanence at last only when the thousands replaced the hundreds, and when large holdings in the hands of a few, whose tenure might be attacked, were supplemented by a maze of individual stakes impossible to unravel. Those officers who requested troops to expel intruders upon Indian reserves in Kansas, calling attention to the "plighted faith" of the United States in the treaties, found the pull of the soil stronger than philosophy and the pressure of the masses more telling in Washington than the letter of the law. The pressure of settlers was central to the removal of the Kansas tribes, and it grew in strength from the lands it fed on and the victories it won, from the Leavenworth confrontation of the 1850s forward.

In 1863 Indians still held almost four million acres in the state, and white residents complained that their area cracked under "the oppressive load," which crippled cities and towns. The general government, it was written, owed it to Kansas to extinguish the Indian title completely, not just gain concessions for traders, land speculators, and railroad men. This should be done even if it required that military colonies be established within the tribes, both for the purpose of providing a nucleus for towns and to force the savages to become civilized. In 1855 observers could still report that when some tribes were told of "great villages covering miles of space . . . and of wigwams built of stone, one on the other . . . and of long trains of wagons that run without horses . . . and of guns that throw balls as large as a man's head," they thought these stories to be extravagant romance. This isolation was shattered by the sixties, as settlers spread over the state and the natives gained new insight into the capabilities of the white man. The *Wabaunsee County Herald* noted in 1869 that to the settler the closing of Indian tenure in the state was an end to be sought for reasons beyond immediate gain. There was plenty of land available to be taken under the liberal provisions of the Preemption and Homestead Acts, but the pioneers showed a "decided mania" for settling on Indian lands. It was a passion, a challenge, a game. It seemed that they chose to "trespass, and worry, and litigate expensively, and quarrel; and sometimes fight," in lieu of compromising with the tribal presence and risking a future life of boredom and recrimination. Individually and in the short term these settlers were less formidable than the corporations or the agents, but collectively and in the long run they were a pivotal factor in bringing Indian Kansas irrevocably to an end.[1]

A study of settler interest in Kansas Indian lands must begin with a return to events of the 1850s near Leavenworth, discussed in outline earlier, and end with the great struggle over the Osage lands. The theme of settler interest in Indian lands was introduced in the territorial period upon the Delaware reservation. It picked up variations on the New York, Iowa, Cherokee, Shawnee, and Potawatomi reserves, and built to a crescendo in the mid-seventies with the establishment of the Wichita metropolis at the former western hunting lodge of the Osages.

Leavenworth experienced a boom in the mid-fifties, the like of which had seldom been recorded upon a frontier and never in Kansas. The secret was money, and the key to the money was the substantial government spending combined with the availability for sale of the Delaware trust lands. Claims to city lots sold for up to $2,000 in 1856, a skilled laborer could earn $4 a day, and it was estimated that $5,000,000 circulated at one time among potential buyers. Each month $30,000 in gold was brought into the region through the government payroll alone, meaning that the support of troops and agents dispatched to protect the Indian from illegal intruders provided these intruders with a good deal of the capital needed to make such protection meaningless. One thinks immediately of the use of tribal trust funds for investment in railroad securities, and there are other examples of the capitalization of Indian resources to support the invaders.[2]

The point has been mentioned earlier that the military not only provided some of the cash but some of the key personnel in the intrusion scheme at Leavenworth. Commissioner George Manypenny believed that nearly every soldier at Fort Leavenworth was involved in buying and selling Indian lands. When the attorney general of the United States ruled that the ceded Delaware lands were not open to settlement, these men hired a lawyer to write a brief defending settlers' rights to move in before the survey. In it, this attorney assumed that the complete removal of Indians from the state was inevitable. He thought that a delay while waiting for a survey would only cause settlers to move to other regions and place the Leavenworth area at a disadvantage in the economic boom that would result from the departure of the tribes. Even the Delawares would be damaged, as the best they could hope for now was a high price for their lands, something which rapid settlement would ensure. But settlers did not wait for a reply to this argument. A writer for the *Kansas Herald* in September, 1854, reported that he had been eager for a Delaware lands homestead, where weeds and flowers grew "with a luxury that can't be described," but he found that men were already building cabins and most of the claims were taken. The next month, the *National Intelligencer* in Washington got a similar report:

> Every stream and every piece of timbered land is now dotted with log cabins, and city lots are freely offered for sale, even as far west as the Republican Fork, near Ft. Riley. Passing over a spot where I had encamped on my outward trip a year previous, I observed long lines of stakes driven in the ground. . . . I inquired the cause of it, and was informed that I had just passed through the courthouse square, and was at that moment entering the Broadway of an embryo Kansas City.

If there were steam mills, hotels, and dwellings upon land still belonging to the Delawares, wrote "A Missourian" in the *National Intelligencer,* it would only enhance the price the Indians would receive "and nobody will be injured." Kansas contemporaries regarded any misunderstanding as the fault of the federal government, which naïvely expected eager settlers "whose Eldorado is always ahead of them" to wait for three months while news of the exact terms of the Delaware treaty, complete with its prohibition upon settlement of ceded lands, reached the West.[3]

Investigation showed the impossibility of separating enforcer from citizen here, as the role of the military became clear. Sackfield Maclin, the paymaster at Fort Leavenworth, and E. A. Ogden, the quartermaster, enraged Manypenny with denials that they had done anything improper with regard to Indian lands. Manypenny said that on a trip to Kansas in the fall of 1854 he had seen a plat of the town of Leavenworth in the backroom of the fort quartermaster's officer, the lots marked for sale. On the door of a large stone warehouse at the fort was a poster advertising a great lot sale for October 9. This bill claimed that the steamers *Polar Star* and *Clara* would be at the river landing to bring in buyers and that the land sale money would be held at St. Louis for possible refund until perfect title arrived from the U.S. Ogden had very early knowledge that the boundaries of the fort reserve were to be reduced, thus leaving a no-man's land between the former boundaries and the Delaware reserve which might be available for a town site. His explanation was that a "Virginia gentleman," "the name of whom wild horses could not pry from him," had visited the Indian Office in Washington, found the original survey of the fort and reserve, located the marker in Kansas, and noticed the discrepancy. Others among the twenty-eight town incorporators (all but the two officers being residents of Missouri) indicated that it was tradition that fort boundaries be a league or a cannon shot from the flagpole, about three miles. This had been accepted by the Indians, so that withdrawal to the actual survey boundary of 1834, two miles from the flagpole, would leave one mile open for settlement. Besides, news of the treaty was delayed, and high Washington officials had written to their constituents while the Kansas-Nebraska Act was being debated, suggesting that they get into the preemption business on the ground floor. Last, there was the law of July 22, 1854, which apparently opened all ceded Indian lands for preemption. Although the actual Delaware treaty stated this rule would not apply to that reserve, the settlers, "not being profound lawyers," concluded that a way would be found to reconcile the two documents, and proceeded with their plans.[4]

Manypenny was much annoyed. He believed he could prove that Maclin, in September, 1854, had offered to sell a preemption claim near the fort to an Ohio man who was told, when he asked about title, that proper influences were being brought to bear and the treaty would be changed. There was no "Virginia gentleman," so far as Manypenny knew, and if anyone had visited Washington on an errand regarding the fort boundaries he had rifled the Indian Office files without official authorization. More likely, the potential town-siters had gone with Major Ogden to see John McCoy, the original surveyor. McCoy told Manypenny that Ogden had requested from him a copy of his original notes, which McCoy provided when Ogden promised he would allow no copies to be made. Manypenny regarded as "cool presumption" the argument that the terms of the treaty were not known, or that its intent with regard to preemption was confused by the July 22 law. The officers' scheme was under way before the passage of the Kansas-Nebraska Act in May, and much before the treaty and the July 22 law were enrolled in the statute books. The Delaware chiefs, returning from Washington, gave public notice of the treaty terms, as did the Delaware agent, on instructions from Washington. The Missouri papers published the substance of it in late May, even before it was signed. Meanwhile, soldiers were employed to build preemption shanties and to cut brush, and government tents were used to shelter squatters. Manypenny admitted that during this time the military did on occasion pursue its duty of driving off squatters, but only such as were not involved in the fort scheme. What a travesty, the commissioner complained, that these acts should have been committed by soldiers, thus sullying the reputation of the government permanently in the minds of the Delawares. "The first violators of law and order—the first to trample on the rights of others—their example has the most pernicious influence, the effects of which are but too visible in the territory." The Delaware agent expressed himself more mildly, but to the same point: "It seems as if the military of the government did not appreciate the object of their organization and establishment on this frontier."[5]

The settlers were not intimidated in the least by these accusations. Wrote "Justice" in the *Kansas Herald:* "Mark, unless the Hon. Commissioner backs down from his position, we will write his obituary as a placeman and politician within a hundred days." Major Ogden called attention also to the pressure of simple numbers. He was voted into the town association, he claimed, without his knowledge, but could see no reason why the settlers should not have their way. "My happiness does not depend upon the success or failure of the town of Leavenworth; but the idea of turning out of house and home, in the midst of cold weather, without any other arrangements. . . several thousand families is shocking to humanity." The history of settler intrusion well into the twentieth century was to indicate that when it came to public attitudes about turning people away from Indian lands it was always winter, and the act was always cruel. Without preemption, went another common line of argument, the country would be in the hands of monopolists and bereft of that guarantee of true Americanism, the small yeoman farmer. Last, and most telling, there came the point that the federal government could hardly expect strict compliance with the rules on the part of the "squatter sovereign" when its policies toward the Indian were filled with deceptions. As a Kansan put it: "In this progressive age, when treaties and compromises are so lightly esteemed, what could the government say to people—simply practising a lesson so flagrantly taught them? Could squatters—the sovereign people—be driven off under a treaty which government—the people's servants—had made and set at naught?" Nothing should interfere with the power of the people, the squatters cried. If the Delaware treaty had a clause preventing slavery, it would be to no avail because the people were obligated to decide. If the Delawares were "rendered needy" by the indifference of their agent and the military in expelling intruders, it must nevertheless be accepted that "these persons in the government employ are themselves of the people," and so could speculate if speculation were the tone of the times. Leavenworth in a year grew from a brush patch to a town of two hundred houses and a thousand residents.[6]

The first sale of Delaware lands in late November, 1856, drew nearly four thousand bidders and resulted in the cohesive settler party getting land at the modest appraised valuation or lower on every occasion. Payment was made in gold and silver, which led to a thriving loan business in bullion at 25 percent to 40 percent interest. All attempts to bring in speculators from the East, including a rumor that pro-slave men were organizing to defeat free-soil settlers, were thwarted by settler claims groups, with the result that the average price was little over the preemption price of $1.25, and this only upon the choicest lands, the rest remaining unsold. "A True Friend of the Delawares" editorialized in a Leavenworth weekly that the Indians would have profited more if they had accepted 85¢ an acre from the U.S. government for the entire reserve, as was once a possibility, or a similar figure from a railroad. Selling to settlers meant that the survey costs would be charged to the Indians, only portions sold, and their income thus diminished. The *National Intelligencer* at Washington came to similar conclusions: Competition in the bidding would have resulted in higher prices, but pressure was brought by town-site and settler associations to insure that this competition was not encouraged by those operating the sale. Some years later one of those in charge remembered:

> Never before was there such a combination and complication of adverse circumstances attending the . . . sales of lands as existed at this particular juncture. It was immediately succeeding the exciting events of 1856, when the entire territory was in a state of revolution and bloodshed . . . . Formidable combinations were made to prevent the lands from being sold to the highest bidder, as the treaty required; and these combinations came very near breaking up the sales at several different times.

Small wonder that most Indian tribes came to prefer purchase of their reserves by railroad companies to this.[7]

By May of 1857 Leavenworth was described as "fast country." The town by then had four thousand residents, and rooms rented for $35 a month. The Delawares, meanwhile, had begun to perceive that the settler wedge would inevitably lead to the sale of their entire reserve and removal from the state. Two of them wrote to President James Buchanan in 1858 that whole tracts of Indian land were being stripped of timber by settlers on the adjacent ceded lands, and that many simply set up housekeeping on Indian tracts. Initially, these people were very humble, explaining they only wished the first chance to purchase should the Indians sell out. If they were given no hope they began to cut and sell timber. They make threats to kill us, said the Delawares, and come around our houses in companies at night: "Even poor widows are not exempt from their broodish avarice." "Instead of . . . protection in the law we thereby became the victims of the lawless." All appeals to Washington had failed, wrote the Indians: "In the length & breadth of the land our kindred is abused harassed & wronged." Nor did this situation change in the next ten years, as new treaties were negotiated, railroads were built, and removal was begun.

The complaints of settler pressure and harassment, keeping the Indian always on edge and receptive to any deal to allow his escape, had been constant. Joseph Bourassa, himself involved in speculation from inside several tribes, complained in 1866 that the Indians could not even take direct and forceful action against these leeches for fear of violating the intercourse laws. "It does seem to me," he concluded, "the course taken in settling our affairs, being so slow, is enough to encourage horse thieves, and lead men to persist in breaking the law." The psychological effect of the Indians' innumerable individual experiences with settlers helps as much as descriptions of intratribal and corporate machinations, to explain the loss of their hold on Kansas.[8]

The situation as perceived by the squatters was well summarized by the Delaware agent, when he wrote in 1855: "These Indians . . . have witnessed and experienced enough to shake their confidence in the laws which govern the white, or perhaps I should say civilized race." The chief of the New York Indians thought that it was a strange reward for ten years of trying to farm and mind their own business that his tribe should be subjected to threats by white squatters with guns. By 1860 the squatters on the New York reserve numbered 2,202, while there were only 50 New York Indians there. The agent for the Iowas reported in 1855 that the settlers had the upper hand in his district: "Men are so constituted that many improper acts are committed by them when combined in associations that few or any would do in the capacity of individuals." The agent, however, admitted that he himself had become involved in town-site speculation at Iola, partly because he was afraid of losing his job with the Indian Office when a new administration was elected in Washington. This interest had prevented him from dealing effectively with ruffians who he said were shooting Iowa Indians on the Great Nemaha reserve with impunity. On the Shawnee lands, tribesman Paschal Fish organized a town site, while a white settler there wrote to his congressman, asking that his "Friends will save me from being cheated out of my claim, by a set of Rascally Copperheads such as Geo. B. Manypenny." On the Sac and Fox reserve claims clubs were formed to keep outsiders off, according to the Delaware model. Thomas Murphy wrote in 1868 that this had so demoralized the Indians under his supervision that they had turned to drink in large numbers, and annuity payments were difficult to distribute due to Indians "shouting and cutting indiscriminately, knocking down all who came in their way no matter who they were." Settlers responded in kind, so as not to be, as one of them put it to President Lincoln, sent "houseless into the wilderness."[9]

These events set the scene for great battles between major contenders for the spoils of Kansas Indian removal: the settlers and the railroads. The railroad won the prize in the Cherokee Neutral Land struggle, while the settlers' interest prevailed in the fight over the Osage lands. Neither victory resulted in the boon for the Indian both adversaries promised. Rather, the proceedings in both cases, lasting from the end of the Civil War into the early seventies, simply gave the tribesmen more evidence of the ruthlessness of all claimants, making tribal tenure at new homes in Indian territory insecure before the Native American immigrants from Kansas were fairly settled.

Kansas City was by 1865 calling itself the "new Babylon," and hoped to justify its claim as a center by building a north-south railroad trunk there. The Kansas & Neosho Valley railroad company was so small it shared an office with a doctor in Olathe, and it showed little promise of reaching Fort Scott, Kansas, much less the Gulf of Mexico. There was, however, the opportunity to grasp capitalized Indian land, the traditional enlivener of moribund frontier enterprises.

Late in 1865, the year of the railroad's organization, its president, Kansas Citian Kersey Coates, and its attorney, a locally famous Civil War hero, James Blunt, attended meetings of the Cherokee Council at Tahlequah, Indian Territory, in hope of obtaining a land grant from the tribe. Although nothing came of this, the railroad board was so impressed with the possibilities that Coates and Blunt were authorized to go to Washington and organize "powwows" with Indian delegations there. Their campaign was remarkably successful. They solicited the aid of Chicago, Burlington & Quincy railroad president James F. Joy, both by allowing him into the inner circle of a group of Kansas City real-estate speculators and by tempting him with the possibility of the road's buying at a fine price the 800,000-acre Cherokee Neutral Tract in the southeast corner of Kansas. Joy, Coates, and Blunt were able to obtain for the railroad in the hectic years immediately following the Civil War not only the Cherokee Neutral Tract at $1.00 an acre but also a federal land grant extending through the Indian Territory to the south of Kansas. This was contingent upon their reaching the southern boundary of Kansas before competing railroads, but the former was a clear gain which the K. & N.V. lobby almost succeeded in having written into the 1866 Cherokee treaty itself. As it was, the competing bidders for the Cherokees' Kansas land had little chance against the political influence Joy was able to muster. The Cherokees had to accept $800,-000 instead of the $12,000,000 they asked for, but they decided that this was the soul of wisdom in light of the fact that the Joy interests threatened, should the Indians balk, to press through legislation making Oklahoma a U.S. territory and thus compromise Cherokee sovereignty over their southern reserve as well as their Kansas holdings. In 1868, with a balance in the company treasury of $8.00, James Joy was elected managing director of the railroad, the name was changed to Missouri River, Fort Scott & Gulf, and construction into the former Cherokee lands was begun.[10]

It seemed to be a standard railroad Indian reserve purchase, such as was so common in the late sixties. Joy happily estimated that revenues from selling this land, combined with income from bonds voted by towns along the way, would exceed the cost of building the railroad to Galveston by $2,000,000—a tidy profit, without one day of operation. Competitors had been neatly diposed of. Four railroads and one land company made bids for the Cherokee Neutral Tract. Coates wrote Joy from Washington that these offers must never leave the office of the secretary of the Interior, lest they "demoralize the Indians . . . and raise the price upon us." One offer, made by the American Emigrant Aid Company, reached the final stages of approval before Secretary James Harlan resigned and was replaced by Orville Browning. Coates found Browning haunted by "fear of public clamor and the possibility of a Congressional Investigation Committee," but the Kansas railroad got from him what it wanted. The sale contract for the Cherokee Kansas lands was signed in October, 1867. Joy's argument had been that his offer was superior to other higher offers because he would pay cash immediately, while other companies wanted terms. When, however, he had the contract in hand, a supplemental treaty with the Cherokees was negotiated in 1868, specifying the same time-payment terms that had been attacked by Joy as unfair to the tribe when proposed by the American Emigrant Aid Company. President Andrew Johnson signed this supplemental treaty, partly because some of James Joy's good friends were prominent among those members of Congress opposed to Mr. Johnson's impeachment. There had seldom been a more tight-knit ring, even among those masterpieces of circularity the Kansas Indian situation generated.[11]

When moving to take advantage of this coup, however, the M.R.F.S. & G. ran into one last barrier—the settlers. Several militant settler organizations, known collectively as the Cherokee Neutral Land League, demanded that the former Indian land be sold to them at the preemption price of $1.25 an acre, rather than the higher price the railroad was likely to charge. They drew up a "death line," south of Fort Scott at the northern boundary of the Neutral Tract, and threatened that any railroad man attempting a survey there would be hanged by a vigilante committee. Violence in the area ranged from the boycott of stores to whippings and substantial property destruction, resulting finally in the calling out of troops by the governor of Kansas to protect the railroad builders.[12]

Although the *Manifesto of the People of the Cherokee Neutral Lands in Kansas* was a radical-sounding document, pledging to do away with the "power of aristocracy and landlordism and railroad kings," Joy found that free passes and other favors went a long way to calming the action, if not the rhetoric, of league leaders and politicians on the local and national level. This fact, and the presence of the troops, made the actions of the hooded nightriders of the Kansas "Balkans" less than determinative. Therefore a court case, *Holden* vs. *Joy,* was entered on behalf of the settlers' league, claiming that it was illegal for the federal government to transfer Indian land directly to companies, thus bypassing federal public domain land laws such as the Preemption and Homestead which would make the land available on easier terms. At the insistence of settler lobbyists, bills were introduced into the Congress to nullify the Joy purchase upon similar grounds. The case reached the Supreme Court of the United States, but the decision in *Holden* vs. *Joy,* reached in 1872, was that the sale of the neutral tract was valid and that Joy had a perfect title. Bills in the Congress to uphold the settlers' view failed. In a last sweep of violence, a gang of leaguers burned the offices of the pro-Joy *Fort Scott Press,* and then settled down and either bought land from the railroad or left the area altogether. The so-called Cherokee Neutral War seemed to confirm strongly that railroad purchase of Indian reserves would be the standard procedure as the tribes were removed from the state, and that the inroads made by the settler interest on the Delaware lands served only to convince governmental officials that transfer to railroads was quicker and cleaner.[13]

Yet, compared with the magnitude of the pressure the settlers were able to apply and their infinite flexibility in trickling through some new crack in the leaky defense of

Indians in Kansas, the Cherokee Neutral loss was as a slap on the nose to a grizzly bear. Whole file cabinets in Washington were filled with sad stories from Cherokee Neutral settlers, including that of a man whose wife was driven to "Puerperal insanity" by the vagaries of title connected with the land boom in Kansas. Already, in 1860, Indian commissioner A. B. Greenwood had dealt with the settlers demanding privileges on the Cherokee Neutral Lands not even ceded by treaty until six years later. The argument was then pushed as hard by the settlers in that area as it had been in other areas when there was some legal basis for settler complaint. The grounds were simply that the Indians were not using the land, and the white man had a right to take it. "However much my sympathy may be involved in behalf of those who are regarded almost as my neighbors," Greenwood had then written, "still the law is imperative and must be obeyed." Despite this and despite Greenwood's certain knowledge that there was a large amount of vacant land elsewhere in Kansas available for settlement, he was hesitant in denying the settler even then: "It is unpleasant for me to occupy a position antagonistic to what the hardy pioneer regards as his legal or equitable claims, or claims based upon supposed rights."[14] How much stronger these "supposed rights" became when actual cession treaties were negotiated can well be imagined. The failure of the Cherokee Neutral Land League did not prevent similar organizations from being formed upon the Miami and Osage reserves. These found "willing advocates on the floor of Congress, in the press, and on the stump." Yet to John Robideaux, head chief of the Miamis, all their arguments narrowed to pure interest. He found eighteen former soldiers among the four hundred pleading for settlement rights on the Miami reserve, while all were claiming to have suffered for their country and to be therefore entitled to compensation in Indian land.

> They claim to have been soldiers, and suffered for their country. Would that give them any extra privilege to rob us of our inheritance? We think not. Much is said about the hardships endured by

the old settler. How is it with us? Were we not forced, years ago, to remove to this land, and told by the Government this was to be our future home forever? How many of our fathers and mothers lie buried along the streams and on the hill tops? How many of our children sleep quietly beneath the trees that shade our homes?

Equally righteous were the settlers. Wrote one who was barely literate but aware of the situation: "If the treaty is nothin and Join Resulation Nothin nor none of the laws Enything but what the grate Interpreter Chuse I pra almity God to pore out his Rath upon such intill men will doo Justis—Justis is all we want."[15]

Upon the Osage lands, the issue of settlers' justice reached its maximum pitch. Here over 8,000,000 acres were at stake, the largest and the last major reserve in the state. The Osage treaty of September 29, 1865, ceded over 4,000,000 acres of this land—844,000 outright for $300,000, and $3,200,-000 in trust to be sold for the benefit of the Indians. The treaty stated specifically that the ceded land was not to be subject to homestead or preemption, nor were school lands set aside, as was the standard requirement with the public domain. While this was being ratified, William Sturges, president of the Leavenworth, Lawrence & Galveston railroad attempted to buy the whole tract, not just the ceded portions, on behalf of his company. In this, he had the help of the James Joy lobby, since Joy effectively controlled the L.L. & G., paralleling the M.R.F.S. & G. to the west, and was as eager for the Osage lands as he was for the Cherokee Neutral Tract. This lobby managed to ensure that government negotiating commissions rejected more favorable offers from other companies and encouraged the Osages to negotiate a new treaty, remove from the state altogether, and sell all their lands to the L.L. & G. In an 1868 draft treaty, negotiated at the junction of Drum Creek and the Verdigris River, the railroad got the right to buy 8,000,000 acres of Osage lands for 20¢ an acre in time payments, no cash being immediately required. During the fifteen years the company had to pay, the land would be exempt from taxation. The settlers were shut out entirely unless they chose to buy from the railroad. Settlers and their representatives in the Congress quickly and loudly cried fraud, which precipitated a battle to stop confirmation of the 1868 treaty by the Senate. A settlers' protective association was formed upon the Osage lands; the settlers were determined not to lose this larger plum in the manner they had lost so many other Indian tracts in the state to rail corporations. Joining the protest were six rival railway companies which had lost their chance through the late treaty negotiations.[16]

Partly because impeachment proceedings against President Johnson occupied the attention of the administration, and partly because Joy's troubles on the neutral tract were enough to keep him busy, the ratification of the 1868 treaty selling to the L.L. & G. was first delayed and then dropped when the Congress, in March, 1871, by legislative fiat, ended Indian treaty-making once and for all. Also active in achieving this result were Sidney Clarke, a member of Congress from Kansas, and congressional land reformers such as George Julian and William Lawrence. Lawrence charged that the railway conspirators were trying to rush the 1868 treaty through by claiming that unless the Osages were immediately removed bloodshed with whites would ensue. This was not any excuse, Lawrence thought, for the Senate and the president "under cover of the treaty-making power" to dictate the land and railroad policy of the country. A congressional committee, upon studying the treaty council proceedings, reported that "the system of bartering immense tracts of Indian lands to railway companies . . . by methods calculated to bar the advance of civilization . . . is too unreasonable to merit serious thought." By February, 1869, a newspaper published at a town near the Osage tract was telling settlers that the 1868 treaty was void and that they should themselves occupy the lands to ensure that the spoils would finally go to the yeoman farmer. Alone in defending the treaty were representatives of the L.L. & G. and government officials. The former pointed out that "a reverse of that decision . . . would not only be out of the line of good precedent, but would also wreck fortunes invested in the faith of the stability of well considered decisions & acts of the Department." The latter maintained that experience with Indian lands in Kansas had shown that it was best to sell lands in a block, good and bad together, and to get the Indians out of the state as rapidly as possible. Offers from other companies had been rejected because the Joy group alone was known for certain to have the means of paying.[17]

Whatever the inclinations of reformers in the Congress, however, it is nearly certain that the railroad sale would have been successful had it not been for incessant pressure from the settlers of the Osage lands. Sidney Clarke, for example, was prone to play both sides of the fence. He had good relations with Joy, although this was not advertised to Kansas farmers, and had expressed the view that the L.L. & G. treaty would be acceptable to him provided the railroad sold the land to settlers for not more than $1.25, thus making itself a profit while increasing the value of the land for its eventual owners through building a transportation link. Clarke changed his view when he received hundreds of letters from settlers indicating what a potent political asset a blanket refusal to deal with "railway monopolists" could be. Clarke learned from settlers' letters that Isaac Kalloch, an officer of the L.L. & G. railroad, was determined to take Clarke's place in the Congress, but that in Kansas the newspaper press was fast turning against Joy, quavering no more at the "impotent threats of the old dotard of Detroit." The settler groups estimated there were 12,000 to 15,000 people upon the Osage lands by 1868. Several Osage land towns, Wichita for example, had applied to the state for incorporation papers despite the absolute illegality of such an action. If the Sturges treaty of 1868 could not be defeated, the settlers wrote, load it down with so many amendments that the railroad would no longer recognize it. The settlers would "fight before they will be driven from their improvements," and Clarke became convinced that "they are all in earnest—some of them terribly in earnest—about this business." It was a very dangerous issue, however. One of Clarke's political advisors told him he had better speak in broad terms and leave himself escape routes, as "all our business men in the country want the road to go through—On the other hand it is a good political hobby to oppose monopolies. It needs careful thought to arrange this matter." Clarke arranged it just right. He proposed substituting the words "State of Kansas" for "Leavenworth, Lawrence & Galveston Railroad Company" in the Sturges treaty. The state would then be bound to sell to settlers at $1.25, but could use the proceeds of the sales to aid "works of internal improvement" (i.e., railroads). "Your land issue," wrote a supporter, "is so broad and takes in collaterally so many winning ideas that you could not have . . . anything better." A man from Wilson County, Kansas, put it more romantically: "Mr. Clarke, the people of Southern Kansas look to you as their Moses to help them out of any difficulty into which they may get regarding these lands."[18]

Clarke's speeches were backed by pamphlets and by such an influx of settlers that the Osage agent said he "might as well try to dam the 'Big Muddy' with a tea spoon" as to try to stop it. George Hoyt, a state lobbyist, responded in 1868 to a pamphlet purporting to explain the Sturges treaty, but signed by I. S. Kalloch, A. N. Blackledge, and William Babcock (all known railroad supporters), with a settler-oriented composition entitled *Kansas and the Osage Swindle*. He called the Sturges treaty "the latest and dirtiest 'job' of the Indian Office," and claimed that several who had been against it at the time of its negotiation had been bribed by the railroad "ring." The Indians were told, wrote Hoyt, that their annuity goods would be withheld until they signed the 1868 treaty, and four barrels of whiskey had been used as positive inducement at Drum Creek. The settlers were eager, it was true, to get the Indians out of the state, but not on such terms as would leave the settler dependent upon terms "dictated by the caprice, cupidity, or necessities of such as may have control of the Leavenworth, Lawrence and Galveston road." The Kickapoo lands, sold to a railroad, were selling for $3.25 an acre, and the Delaware lands were held for prices of $12.00 to $100.00 an acre. So selfish were these corporations that the pending treaties gave not one acre for state schools. Surely the difference between the 20¢ an acre proposed and the $1.25 the settler would pay should be enough to satisfy any speculator, but the railroad would not agree to a fixed price. Hoyt concluded: "The fact is, nothing is intended to-day, nor has been at any previous time since the treaty was drawn in the office of Tom Ewing and agreed to by the various parties in interest, from the Head of the Department down to the gentlemen who sneeze when Mr. William Sturges inhales his snuff, but to circumvent justice and successfully accomplish a huge steal of public lands."[19]

The settler defeat of the Sturges treaty was assured when, on July 15, 1870, the Congress enacted a law providing that the Osage trust lands and diminished reserve (i.e., those lands not absolutely ceded in the *1865* treaty) were to be surveyed and sold to actual settlers only, with the traditional reservations for the support of schools. The Osages approved and agreed to remove entirely from the state. The formal end of treaty-making the next year put further transfer of Indian reserves to railroads through the treaty process forever out of reach.[20]

These decisions, however, did not end railroad prospects for Osage lands nor the settlers' battle against the companies. Both the L.L. & G. and M.K. & T. railroads had been given federal land grants by the Congress, in 1866 and 1863, respectively. The land grant acts had been vaguely worded as to whether the grant extended through Indian land in the event tribal title was extinguished, and so both roads now claimed the 844,000 acres of land in the Osage eastern ceded reserve of 1865 as part of their land grants. The commissioner of the general land office at first declared that the railroads had no such rights, but his decision was reversed by his superior, Secretary of the Interior Orville Browning, who had been so kind to James Joy in reversing a decision to sell the Cherokee Neutral Tract to a Joy competitor in 1866. The Senate backed this view, however much the House complained, and the two railroads began selling parts of the ceded lands as the settlers prepared pamphlets and court cases.[21]

The railroads in this, their last chance at Indian lands in Kansas, made a most determined effort. The Sturges treaty itself was largely the result of lobbying by the L.L. & G., which was authorized by its land-grant legislation to negotiate with Indians for the sale of lands. Since this railroad did not become a major trunk line but ended up as a Santa Fe branch line, it is easy to forget how powerful it was in the 1860s. In addition to the Sturges treaty, the L.L. & G. had managed to bring to the final negotiation stage a treaty with the Cherokees which would have provided it with former Indian lands all the way to the Texas border had its devices succeeded. With the M.R.F.S. & G. in control of the Cherokee Neutral Tract, the Joy railroad system in Kansas was, in the late sixties, the most likely contender for the primary north-south midcontinent railway system. Joy's fate with cautious eastern capitalists was to turn partly upon the manner of his dealing with the vital issue of railroad speculation in Indian lands. A tentative victory upon the neutral lands, yielding a harvest of ill-will, must not be followed by defeat on the Osage tract. The M.K. & T. was similarly earnest, since it was locked with the Joy roads in a struggle for financial backing, and in a construction race to the southern border of Kansas, beyond which Congress had decreed only a single road, the first to arrive, would be allowed to proceed through the tribal lands in Indian Territory. In 1868 it was reported that the president of the M.K. & T. (then called Union Pacific, Southern Branch) was also register of the land office at Humboldt, Kansas, at the north boundary of the Osage lands, though this was obviously a conflict of interest. But his work had been a disappointment to the road, which had also attempted to place one of its officers in the position of agent for the Osage Indians, so better to guarantee its hoped-for land base.[22]

Fortunately, a packet of letters from this period emanating from the L.L. & G. offices remains extant and provides a glimpse of that road's strategy regarding the Osage lands.

Rail president J. M. Walker wrote to Joy's assistant that the L.L. & G. expected to sell its share of the Osage ceded lands at no less than an average of $8.00 an acre, and hoped for $10.00 an acre on about 500,000 acres, no matter what the settler expected. Therefore, getting the patents for the land was most vital, and the L.L. & G. turned to the influential Ewing family for legal counsel rather than to the departments in Washington. Particularly annoying was that on about 20,000 acres the claims of the L.L. & G. and the M.K. & T. overlapped, and the roads were having difficulty working out a division among themselves of a bounty that was not even certainly in hand. Worse, William Lawrence, a senator from Ohio with a budding reputation as a land reformer, was writing effective pamphlets on behalf of the settlers. Also, it was rumored that Senator Samuel Pomeroy of Kansas had influenced the Interior Department to reopen the title case depite the L.L. & G.'s insistence that "a matter which has been two or three times settled officially, judicially and legislatively ought not again to be disturbed." To counter this the M.K. & T. and the L.L. & G. planned to "get control" of several of the leading men of the settler movement, presumably through bribes, and thus quiet the agitation. Also, notice was taken of newspapers that attacked the railroad title and pressure was applied. Wrote Walker to rail attorney Solon O. Thacher: "Cannot you manage to keep [the *Lawrence Journal*] . . . and others in some shape. I do not care about their advocating our title but I prefer they should say nothing on the subject." One thing that did not seem wise was to enter into "political combinations" for the purpose of electing members of the state legislature and congress friendly to the railroad. There was too much danger of this sort of activity being discovered and backfiring, Walker thought.[23]

The best efforts of the Leavenworth, Lawrence & Galveston could not prevent Lawrence's arguments from prevailing late in 1871. The case was reopened by the Interior Department, and Lawrence sent the L.L. & G. a letter advising the railroad to compromise by guaranteeing the settlers a price of $1.25 an acre on any Osage lands granted to the company. Walker wrote Levi Parsons of the M.K. & T. that he was amazed at this, as he thought everything in Washington was arranged. "To have it overthrown this way was not very satisfactory I assure you." Walker's reply to Lawrence's "improvident" letter suggesting compromise was that "it seems to me madness, unless something has occurred of which I am not advised, to talk about compromising . . . on any terms that the settlers could possibly accept and carry out." The railroad proposed to fight. It hired Judge Thacher to prepare briefs. It also immediately began a campaign to have the hearings postponed until after the November elections in Ohio, since Secretary of the Interior Columbus Delano had ambitions to be senator from that state and William Lawrence might be of use to him in accomplishing that goal. Walker admitted to his attorneys that there was "one chance in a thousand" for Lawrence to succeed in having railroad title set aside, although "to do so he must overturn all precedent and law and forget every principle of Justice and right." The rail officers knew that Lawrence was trying to buy the lands from them on his own behalf and then resell them to settlers at increased prices. Wrote one: "Lawrence is a scamp undoubtedly."[24]

To the general public, lacking some of the specific information about his plans, Lawrence seemed a hero. In February, 1872, he had published a stinging attack upon the L.L. & G. and its Osage land claims. If the railroad were successful in the ceded lands, he wrote, its officers would again try to obtain the trust lands, and the settler would be left nothing. He believed that railroad arguments that the land grants included the Osage land were "a forced construction which must shock the legal mind and conscience, and the moral sense of mankind." The time had come to change a policy that always favored the railroad companies and was against the settlers.[25]

Similar rhetoric came from the pen of William Johnston, a settler lobbyist. He claimed that "King" Joy was frightened that the settlers, his underlings, were rising against him, and that "the word *squatter* may come to represent a far better man than the word speculator, or even the title of railroad king." If the government did not protect the settler now, it would "stink in the nostrils of the civilized world." Johnston said that if all the capitalists on Wall Street, Mr. Joy included, were reduced to the condition of the settlers and had to work for an honest living, it would not be so evil as the denial to one of these settlers of his home. He quoted: "Princes and lords may flourish and may fade; / A breath can unmake them as a breath has made; / But a brave peasantry, their country's pride, / If once destroyed can never be supplied."[26]

All rhetoric aside, however, the railroads' claims to land grants in the Osage cession seemed to stand. Clarke's retainers reminded him that he should not go so far with the settlers as to alienate the state businessmen and thus ensure that Isaac Kalloch would represent Kansas in the next legislature. Robert Stevens, now an employee of the M.K. & T., reported to Clarke that even Benjamin Butler and George Julian, reformers who stood publicly against monopoly, were willing to support the railroads in this case. Sticking with the settler cause at this point, wrote L. J. Worden, would mean "all *R.R.* in the state will be solid against you, and that Senator Pomeroy will stand back and see it done rather than assist you." Therefore, even in the face of what was described to him as a "steal" by the M.K. & T. and certain "small thieves" of the Kansa Indian lands around Council Grove, Clarke laid relatively low and the L.L. & G. and M.K. & T. proceeded to sell Osage lands at $2 to $15 an acre. The L.L. & G. was promised by Senator Samuel Pomeroy, himself an investor in Leavenworth lots which would be helped by the railroad's success, that "no scrap of paper shall go through Congress which shall in the slightest affect our interests there." That railroad also made sure that the newspapers it controlled took the position that there was no hope for settlers but to buy from the railroad. When the settlers came to the Humboldt land office to "prove up" on their claims, they met, according to a Topeka newspaper, nothing more yielding than the "metallic front" of a railway agent.[27]

There remained, however, an appeal to the courts, and the settlers took this course even as the railroad companies had begun to relax with the feeling that their position was secure. When the cases involving the M.K. & T. and L.L. & G. title to alternate sections in the Osage lands reached the U.S. Supreme Court in 1875, it found the justices split upon the issue of land monopoly and a majority receptive to the settlers' argument.[28]

The railroads' arguments were written by S. O. Thacher, for the L.L. & G., and T. C. Sears, for the M.K. & T. In 1866, they said, when the treaties and the railroad grants were being ratified, they were regarded as part of one package. As Sears put it:

> The demand and policy were, that the Indian title should be extinguished and the lands . . . or the proceeds thereof should be used in the construction of railroads. . . . By this means the Indians received what was, to them, fabulous sums of money—more than they had ever conceived. The railroad companies realized substantial benefits by way of moneys and credit in the construction of their roads, and the public received and has now the benefit of the railroads.

The intent, the railroad attorneys said, must be interpreted in the light of the designs and objects of the laws as reflected by recent history, a history which was filled with transfers of Indian reserves to railroads according to the pattern Sears described. This pattern, it was argued, was as well understood "as any fact that has transpired within the last eventful fifteen years," and it was therefore hypocrisy for the settler to question it now that he had the chance to have his cake and eat it too. The Indian treaties, if they were to be respected, stated that the railroads should have a chance to buy the Osage lands, and both the state courts and the Department of the Interior had agreed that these land grants, at least, were valid. There was little settlement upon these lands, Thacher noted, and the settlers' argument that two whole counties would be depopulated by "the imperious demands of these corporations" was as "pure a fiction" as the settlers' expression of surprise and shock that an Indian treaty could ever contemplate sale of lands to a railroad. What was happening, the railroad men argued, was simply that there was a change in the political wind. The power was shifting away from the railroads, and therefore this was an attempt by the government to call off all promises to them, even if it meant calling black white with regard to past intentions. Wrote Sears:

> Railway corporations seem to have but very few rights which are tangible, fixed or certain . . . . How long before the same spirit that now wages relentless warfare against them, shall attack other branches of industry and commerce, and seek to cripple other enterprises that demand and employ both capital and trained skill, will depend somewhat upon the success attendant upon its present efforts.

A lesson the Indian had had to swallow long before came home to rest. The Supreme Court decided in favor of the settlers in both cases. Kansas settlers had all the Osage lands at $1.25 an acre.[29]

The eventual victory of the settlers in the Osage controversy did, as the railroads described, represent a definite change of direction in the precedents set for the transfer of Indian lands in Kansas after the disastrous Delaware land auctions of the 1850s. In Kansas it was an anomaly, for the trend came too late to affect most tribes, which were already gone. The Kansas experience, however, with its late surge of settler strength, did have an impact upon the later history of Indian Territory, where the pattern of railroad purchase of Indian reserves never obtained, however much power was gained by corporations through leasing. The L.L. & G. and M.R.F.S. & G. were compelled, partly because lobbying for Indian lands had slowed their progress in the border construction race, to languish forever in the backwater of Kansas intrastate railroads, while the M.K. & T., pushing on south into the Indian Territory, was no more able to collect its contingent land grant there than it had been to sweep in the Osage ceded lands to the north. The tribes in the mid-seventies were settled on reserves in Indian Territory in a situation, except for crowding, much like that of Kansas in 1854. There they would await the administration of the new techniques that enterprise would eventually develop to seal their total doom. Meanwhile, in Kansas, the last tribal remnants were harried out of the state by the victors eager for the spoils. The matter of the use of former Indian reserves, wrote George Crawford to James Joy, was now "beyond the control of the leaders and in the hands of the people."

In the last battle, the boomer had acquired lands—previously guaranteed to the Indians, and serviced by railroads—at the preemption price of unsurveyed wilderness. The state's populist tendencies were given a rousing lift.[30]

CHAPTER SIX

And Then
There Were None

LEAVING KANSAS required of the tribes a terribly difficult psychological adjustment, since many of them were being torn from established homes for the second time in thirty years. Ottawa chief John Wilson repeated over and over as he walked south to Indian Territory that he did not want to go. He died on the road of a chill contracted while trying to catch some of his horses in a rainstorm. The last of the Modocs from California came through Kansas City in railroad cars, painted black in mourning for the dead. Newspaper reporters commented on the "peculiar odor" arising from the crouched Indians on the way to their last home. So reluctant were the Potawatomi Indians to leave the state that they refused in 1870 to have a census taken to enumerate those to be removed. From the end of the Civil War forward, Kansas newspapers applauded the demise of the Native American "vagabonds and thieves," who had kept the best lands of Kansas from the settlers, and largely missed the tragedy of their going. "I feel," said one Indian, "as if I were standing on the end of a log, and a very light one too, which is floating on water one hundred feet deep, and that the log is liable at any moment to turn over with me and drown me." Said a representative of a Kickapoo delegation

133

in Washington, after the usual ceremonies and an explanation of their "new life" by officials: "We accept the flags, but they will not support these children. . . . I could not sleep last night—all of these Indians here cried."[1]

After 1866 Kansas and the federal government moved rapidly toward carrying out a removal which had a well-developed strategy. Samuel Crawford, wartime governor of Kansas, was consistently charged by the Osage agent in particular with attempting to use the state militia to frighten the tribes, provoke them to hostility, and thus provide an excuse for their more rapid movement to the south. This pressure was paralleled by a rapid sale to settlers of Indian lands ceded in trust, almost one and a half million acres between 1864 and 1868, thus allowing settlers to apply additional pressure before the tribes had time to pack. Lewis Bogy, commissioner of Indian Affairs, wrote to the House Committee on Indian Affairs in December of 1866 that it was time for the Kansas Indians to move on for the last time, as "their present location is of very great injury to the white race, and is also very bad for the Indians." His object, he said, was to negotiate treaties of removal with all of them and to get them to Indian Territory "where I believe they would be much happier." Men in the state were more certain still. There was a proposal in 1868 to move the southern boundary of the state one-half degree south to take over some Indian Territory land occupied by small tribes (Quapaws, Shawnees, Senecas)—the home, in the language of a concurrent resolution of the Kansas legislature, "only of the savage whose ideas of advancement and improvement are wholly and totally inadequate to the profitable cultivation and improvement of this most beautiful country." A settler of the Potawatomi reserve held in 1870:

> . . . the right of occupancy, the right to occupy some space on Earth while they exist, is the only right to land that has ever been acceded in Indian treaties by civilized people. . . . The Indians are not an independent people. . . . The government of the U.S. should cease to use its bayonets to turn back the

process of civilization. . . . There is an irrepressible
conflict existing between civilization and barbarism.
The government should not try to uphold both.

In 1871, the secretary of the Interior noticed that for the
first time since the presidency of George Washington no
appropriation had been passed for the striking of Indian
peace medals. Vincent Colyer, after a talk with Kansas representative Sidney Clarke, wrote to another member of the
reform-oriented Board of Indian Commissioners: "The
more I see of the Indian business the more confused it becomes. I can only get satisfaction by turning to the Saviour
and with faith remember that he can bring it all to a good
result. I have no doubt but that with his blessing we shall
yet see order and justice come out of the chaos and wrong."[2]

To the tribes, trusting in the Holy Spirit alone seemed
a practice without good credentials in their past experience.
Their strategy for dealing with the chaos overtaking them
therefore had its active side. The Sacs and Foxes refused to
dispatch delegates to select lands for their new homes to the
south and destroyed timber in order to deny it to settlers
moving in. The result was that Keokuk, the established chief,
was suspended and replaced by government chief Ne-graw-ho.
As will be recalled, Thomas Murphy noted that "unless Keokuk is given a set back by the Dept. he will ride rough shod
over his agent and everybody else, paying no attention to the
wishes or instructions of government officials." This could
have a "demoralizing" effect on other tribes, encouraging
them also to resist removal. However, even when in November, 1869, the bands of four Sac and Fox chiefs left their
Kansas homes "in good spirits," one, Mo-ko-ho-ko, declined
to go. He was rumored plotting with the Prairie Band of
Potawatomis to organize a last ditch resistance by full-bloods.
The Prairie Band in fact continued to refuse all attempts to
bribe them with allotments or annuities to remove. They
held to their property "with great tenacity," according to
their agent, and managed to remain in the state to the present
day, despite their agency buildings being occupied by squatters in the early seventies, and despite an 1872 ruling by

Secretary of the Interior Delano that the Potawatomi Nation was "extinct." The Delawares also delayed in selecting Indian Territory land, and their situation was complicated by the reluctance of the Cherokees and other Indians, resident in Indian Territory only since the last removal, to give up their lands and adjustment in order to settle these new exiles. In the arguments back and forth, the Delawares feared, like the other Kansas tribes, that they would, in losing their homes, lose their identity and the last of their pride as well. Wrote their chief Fall Leaf to Washington in 1867: "We call ourselves Delaware Indians. Before the Government of the United States was formed, we were a nation, and for time to come, as far as human mind can conceive, we wish to be a nation. We trust in God." Too many sovereign nations with conflicting goals were soliciting God's help in Kansas for the Deity to satisfy everyone, while the whites mustered more earthly forces in helping themselves.[3]

If it were not by this time obvious to all where the power lay, the last months of Indian Kansas were filled with a spectacle of suffering which should have roused pity in the hardest heart. Thomas Murphy reported in 1869 that some Indians under his control were living on roots and nuts, and that starvation was widespread among tribes waiting to be provided with a home. Scattered warfare was reported—for example, seven Pawnees were killed in a fight near Ellsworth —but this was most generally connected with the climax of the Indian wars to bring nomadic Plains tribes to bay and was not connected with the project of removal of the sedentary groups who claimed Kansas as a homeland. The latter simply tried as best they could to endure the debilitating experience of losing all for the second time. Fall Leaf of the Delawares recalled in broken English those earlier times, when his tribe had been told that any time they needed something they should simply ask their Father in Washington. We need something now, the chief wrote to the government, some food:

> We do honest want to have it done. Because since 4
> years we have lost what little was left then. and crop

fail, and every Article of the kind we need is very high in price. We wish our Great Father should be kind give such is need Now. even no seed to plant. We should like to have it done right off. for God sake. and Remember the treatys, we hope Government should listen our suffering nation. We Sallute Government and to all braves wise men and all children. God May Bless Us All.

The Sacs and Foxes protested that the whites were literally tearing down Indian houses and hauling away the materials before the occupants had left. The agent there requested troops, which he said he needed to protect Indians harvesting their crops from being shot down by settlers. Those like Mo-ko-ho-ko who were determined to stay took the worst abuse of all. The Sac and Fox agent reported that whites were nightly throwing stones at the doors of members of Mo-ko-ho-ko's band, but that they could not be protected since the government bureaucracy left no one with authority to help those who did not remove with the tribe. Officially, they did not exist. By the time the main body of Sacs and Foxes arrived in Indian Territory in a January snowstorm, in 1870, Mo-ko-ho-ko's band was in desperate shape. Two years later many of its women and children wandered about the Kansas prairies naked and begged to be taken in wherever anyone would have them. In 1879, after a forced removal of this band under military guard in 1876, the whole of Mo-ko-ho-ko's band was back on the old Kansas reserve, reduced to destitute serfs working at odd jobs on the lands of white speculators. But they were at the home of their fathers, and that is where they wanted to stay, whatever the price. The Sac and Fox agent had written in 1869 that "there are enough infernal scoundrels to make this the hottest place in which to do his duty an agent was ever placed." The Indians, it was reported, "look and feel gloomy and down-hearted" and were burdened with wrongs "sufficient to call down upon the state and Nation the wrath of the Great Father of all."[4]

The Kansas removal case that came closest to awakening

the conscience of a nation in a postwar moral slumber was that of the much-maligned Osages. As early as the fall of 1867, just when the treaties granting lands to the L.L. & G. and M.K. & T. railroads were signed, the Osages were known to be in "a deplorable condition." Grasshoppers and drought had wiped out their crops and the marauding Plains Indians prevented them from hunting buffalo. They were driven by hunger to stealing cattle from the trail herds driving to the railhead at Abilene from Texas, which practice added violent retaliation by tough drovers. Whites moving to the Osage reserve stole Indian ponies, and the tribesmen dared not venture after them for fear of their lives. "Must these Indians," wrote their Quaker agent G. C. Snow, "starve and starve and steal and steal with money in the United States treasury?"[5]

The most organized, though ineffective, response to this came from the Board of Indian Commissioners, which had been organized in 1868 as a watchdog agency for Indian affairs. Even though the Osages had "consented" to removal, wrote a member, "They are human beings, they have rights," and should be allowed to remain in peace upon the land given them by treaty until orderly change could be arranged. Why were the Osages starving, the commissioners asked, when the government would soon sell their lands at high prices? Why did the government allow the damages caused by "the invasion of the 'Christians,' " when military force might be used to protect the reserves until settlement was authorized? Why was nothing drastic done when the national press reported in 1871 that one half-blood Osage, Joseph Mosier, a former soldier in the Union Army, had been driven insane by settler harassment and then died? The answer was that the mood of the settlers, who threatened Indians with ax and lynch noose, was largely the mood of the nation. Few were shocked when in 1871 some unarmed Osages near the Kansas line were forced by a party of seventeen whites to dismount and run for their lives while trigger-happy frontiersmen used them for rifle targets. In the summer of 1873 some Osages returning to their Indian Territory agency from a western buffalo hunt drifted across the Kansas line into Barber County, met a party of Kansas militia, and lost five of their number. An investigation revealed that the militia was acting without orders and that there may have been a plan in the state to keep the Indian threat going, as it had served the state so well in the past in getting money for defense and development. Commented one of the Board of Indian Commissioners: "I could not realize the extent of the wickedness of the white men."[6]

Whatever the pain to some white consciences, Indian Kansas did indeed disappear. Where over ten thousand Native Americans had, at the beginning of the Civil War, made their homes, by 1875 fewer than one thousand—the Prairie Band of Potawatomis, a few Kickapoos, and even fewer members of maverick bands of Sacs and Foxes—remained. Where once the state maps were covered with boundaries of Indian reserves, only two small ones were then drawn, and had it not been for Kansas Indian place-names (enough to fill a book-length study), a twentieth-century observer might not guess that any part of the drama of Indian disinheritance was played out here.[7]

Could it have been different? Must it have happened that way? One of the lessons of history is that nothing is inevitable, but another is that, human nature being what it is, subtle exploitation of minority cultures by the majority is to be expected, if not accepted. The few Indian tribes that remained in Kansas demonstrated that only those whose Indianness and tribal nationality were so important to them that they were not tempted by offers of money, railroads, power in the tribe, or other eroding blandishments described in these chapters could resist white expansion. The citizens of the United States in the nineteenth century needed some moral loophole, be it ever so slight, and they salved their collective conscience by believing that the Indian was somehow better off where they finally placed him than he had been whence they took him. They needed to believe that he had "consented," that he had shared in the spoils, that he understood that the process was "for his own good." If all efforts to coerce or tempt him met with blank and uncompromising resistance, if the tribe remained united in its resolve to stick to its traditional culture without modification, there was a limit to how far the white man would push him. Whites would not, as a rule, simply exterminate Indians, with no shadow of a cause. Incidents such as the Sand Creek Massacre of 1864 were fresh in the minds of officials as they dealt with the Kansas removal issue, and they did not, despite isolated contemporary statements or the impression of some books on Indian policy, regard such ruthless slaughter of innocents as something which could be tolerated, much less encouraged. These officials and businessmen were not generally evil in that simple sort of way; they merely believed that they could buy Indian sovereignty and purchase promises in the same way that they made transactions regarding everything else, including Kansas lands. That an Indian might cling to his homeland or his tribal way of communal landholding or the grave of his father at the cost of economic desolation was unimaginable to the "progressive" mentality of the whites, and, as it happened, to the "progressive" mentality of a large number of tribal citizens. Therefore, while removal could have been prevented by a mass nonviolent, noncompromising resistance, such as Mahatma Ghandi used to goad the collective conscience of Englishmen, knowledge of conditions and attitudes among whites and Indians in nineteenth-century Kansas leads to the conclusion that this was hardly to be expected. The Indians were removed largely by severe, though not irresistible, pressure combined with real and illusional temptations so that the exercise of free will became a complex and confusing undertaking.

That such was the case does not, however, prevent the modern student from joining those who, at the time, hoped that leadership somewhere would rise above the level of common expectation to bring about one of those surprising reversals that fill human history with hope. Neither side produced it and, since the whites had so much to gain and nothing to lose, they are most to be blamed for following blindly the inane dictum that the "real 'Native Americans' shall become with us the 'carpetbaggers' one people." They are to be blamed for ignoring a situation which by 1905 had reduced those Prairie Potawatomis who had stayed in Kansas to performing in a mock stage robbery at the "Realistic Wild West" show for tourists at St. Marys, Kansas. They can be censured for naming the state after the Kansa Indians, pushing that tribe out of its boundaries, and then carping about the cost of boxes and suits in which to bury its members. And most of all, they may be taken to task for learning nothing from their own past—they repeated in Kansas the removal policy which had led to such suffering in the East in the 1830s, and again repeated in Indian Territory from the 1870s to 1907 a campaign of temptation, tribal division, and corporate intrusion similar to that mounted in Kansas. "The whole Indian Territory will be in the hands of land speculators & R. Road monopolies in less than ten days," wrote one sensitive observer in 1871, if in fact the government or the private will did not at last check those forces responsible for the sack of Indian Kansas. Apparently responding to evidence that the misplaced Indians were preparing a much firmer resistance to white encroachments in Indian Territory, one perceptive reformer wrote, "I can now see more clearly than ever before the reason for the stubborn tenacity with which the Indians . . . stick to their rights under treaties. I don't know but they are wiser than their best friends in this regard." Taking a hard look at Kansas, largely devoid of the tribes which once had inhabited its plains, prairies, and fertile valleys and now filled with white yeomen whose hustle and bustle were only occasionally interrupted by the sad farewells of its former red population, a federal official could only comment, "It seems as though the D——l had changed his residence, & gone to Kansas, for certainly no such atrocities could be committed without his leadership."[8]

Notes

Abbreviations used in National Archives citations:

F	Frame
GIC-ID, ID	General Incoming Correspondence, Indian Division, Interior Department
LR-ID, ID	Letters Received, Indian Division, Interior Department
LR-OIA	Letters Received, Office of Indian Affairs
M	Microfilm
NA	National Archives
R	Roll
RHR	Record of the United States House of Representatives
RS	Records of the United States Senate
SCLS-ID, ID	Special Classes of Letters Sent, Indian Division, Interior Department

CHAPTER ONE: TERRITORIAL KANSAS
AND THE INDIAN

1. Roy F. Nichols, *The Disruption of American Democracy* (New York, 1948); Paul Wallace Gates, *Fifty Million Acres: Conflicts Over Kansas Land Policy, 1854–1890* (New York, 1966 edition); James C. Malin, *The Nebraska Question, 1852–1854* (Lawrence, 1953); James C. Malin, *Indian Policy and Westward Expansion*, University of Kansas, Humanistic

Studies, *Bulletin*, II, No. 3 (Lawrence, 1921); and Barrington Moore, *Social Origins of Dictatorship and Democracy: Lord and Peasant in the Modern World* (Boston, 1966), Ch. III.

2. Robert F. Berkhofer, Jr., *Salvation and the Savage: An Analysis of Protestant Missions and American Indian Response, 1787–1862* (Lexington, 1965); Gates, *Fifty Million Acres*, 3–10. For the traditional "Bleeding Kansas" theme see Alice Nichols, *Bleeding Kansas* (New York, 1954); Charles Robinson, *The Kansas Conflict* (Lawrence, 1898); J. N. Holloway, *History of Kansas: From the First Exploration of the Mississippi Valley, to its Admission into the Union* (LaFayette, 1868); Charles R. Tuttle, *A New Centennial History of the State of Kansas* (Madison and Lawrence, 1876); A. T. Andreas, *History of the State of Kansas* (Chicago, 1883); William E. Connelley, *A Standard History of Kansas and Kansans*, 5 Vols. (Chicago, 1928); and G. Raymond Gaeddert, *The Birth of Kansas* (Lawrence, 1940).

3. William Phillips, *The Conquest of Kansas, by Missouri and Her Allies* (Boston, 1856), 18. Phillips was a correspondent for the *New York Tribune*. *National Intelligencer* (Washington), June 25, 1857.

4. Charles J. Kappler (comp. and ed.), *Indian Affairs. Laws and Treaties*, II (Washington, 1904), 262–264, 546–549, and *passim;* George A. Schultz, *An Indian Canaan, Isaac McCoy and the Vision of an Indian State* (Norman, 1972), 96–97; and *Congressional Globe*, 33d Cong., 1st Sess., XXIII, Pt. 1, 186.

5. *U.S. Statutes at Large*, X (March 3, 1853), 238–239; Kappler, *Treaties*, II, 218, 222, 416; and Malin, *Nebraska Question*, 128–130.

6. Deposition of Abelard Guthrie, September 12, 1862, Letters Received, Indian Division, Interior Department (hereafter cited as LR-ID, ID) Record Group (hereafter cited as RG) 48, Microfilm (hereafter cited as M) 825, Roll (hereafter cited as R) 20, Frames (hereafter cited as F) 0758–0759, National Archives (hereafter cited as NA); Guthrie to ?, December 26, 1865, Letters Received by the Office of Indian Affairs (hereafter cited as LR-OIA) RG 75, M 234, R 814, F 0878–0879, Shawnee Agency, NA; Guthrie to ?, Spring, 1866, RG 75, M 234, R 814, F 0867–0871, Shawnee Agency, NA; "Papers Concerning the Claim of Abelard Guthrie Against the

Wyandot and Shawnee Indians in Kansas, 1872," RG 48, Special File 83, Box 765, NA.

7. Malin, *Nebraska Question*, 128–136.

8. *Ibid.*, 133–134; *Independence* (Missouri) *Reporter*, September 7, 1853, cited in Malin, *Nebraska Question*, 134; *Missouri Democrat* (St. Louis), June 30, August 13, October 18, and November, 1853.

9. *National Intelligencer*, November 5, 1853; and Gates, *Fifty Million Acres*, 18–19.

10. *Missouri Democrat*, August 27, 1853, June 28, 1854; Malin, *Nebraska Question*, 142–143. See also William E. Parrish, *David Rice Atchison of Missouri, Border Politician* (Columbia, 1961), *passim*.

11. *Missouri Democrat*, April 17, 1853.

12. For the Manypenny treaties of 1854 with the Otoes, Missouris, Delawares, Shawnees, Iowas, Sacs and Foxes, Miamis, Wyandots, and the United Kaskaskias, Peorias, Piankeshaws, and Weas, see Kappler, *Treaties*, II, 609–681. Significantly, none of these treaties were proclaimed until after the Kansas-Nebraska Bill became law on May 30, 1854. *Congressional Globe*, 33d Cong., 1st Sess., XXIII, Appendix, 153, 345–346, 636; and *Congressional Globe*, 33d Cong., 1st Sess., XXIII, Pt. 1, 187.

13. *Missouri Democrat*, February 7, 1854; *Congressional Globe*, 33d Cong., 1st Sess., XXIII, Pt. 1, 275.

14. *U.S. Statutes at Large*, X (May 30, 1854), 277; Manypenny to McClelland, September 29, 1855, General Incoming Correspondence, Indian Division, Interior Department (hereafter cited as GIC-ID, ID), RG 48, Box 4, NA; Robinson to Alexander Cumming, October 30, 1854, *House Executive Document No. 50*, 33d Cong., 2d Sess. (Serial 783), 38, quoting an article that first appeared in the *Parkville* (Missouri) *Seminary;* and George W. Ewing to Andrew Jackson (Potawatomi Indian), March 13, 1854, *Annual Report of the Commissioner of Indian Affairs* (1855), 230.

15. *U.S. Statutes at Large*, X (July 22, 1854), 310; Manypenny to McClelland, August 8, October 25, 1854, GIC-ID, ID, RG 48, Box 4, NA; *Kansas Weekly Herald* (Leavenworth), September 15, 1854; George C. Whiting to Franklin Pierce, October 21, 1854, McClelland to Pierce, November, 1854,

LR-ID, ID, RG 48, M 825, R 2, F 0047–0049, NA; and Gates, *Fifty Million Acres*, 48–49, 112–113.

16. *Annual Report of the Commissioner of Indian Affairs* (1854), 10; *National Intelligencer*, July 17, 1857; and *Kansas Weekly Herald*, July 31, 1858.

17. B. F. Robinson to Alexander Cumming, June 10, 1855, LR-OIA, RG 75, M 234, F 0019–0020, Delaware Agency, NA; Manypenny to McClelland, January 6, 1855, GIC-ID, ID, RG 48, Box 2, NA; McCaslin to Cumming, December 7, 20, 1855, LR-OIA, RG 75, M 234, R 645, F 0045, 0078, Osage River Agency, NA; McClelland to Commissioner of Indian Affairs, October 5, 1855, Selected Classes of Letters Sent to Indian Division, Interior Department (hereafter cited as SCLS-ID, ID), RG 48, M 606, R 2, F 0148, NA; McCaslin to Cumming, June 23, 1856, LR-ID, ID, RG 48, M 825, R 1, F 0212–0213, NA; and A. B. Greenwood to S. M. Burrough, March 7, 1860, Records of the House of Representatives (hereafter cited as RHR), RG 233, Packet HR 36AOD11.4, NA.

18. B. M. Crust *et al.* to Manypenny, August 2, 1854, cited in *House Executive Document No. 50, 33d Cong., 2d Sess.* (Serial 783), 42. For the general relationship between yeomanry, democracy, and the assault on the public domain see Henry Nash Smith, *Virgin Land: The American West as Symbol and Myth* (Cambridge, 1950), Leo Marx, *The Machine in the Garden, Technology and the Pastoral Ideal in America* (New York, 1964), Bernard W. Sheehan, *Seeds of Extinction: Jeffersonian Philanthropy and the American Indian* (Chapel Hill, 1973), and Roderick Nash, *Wilderness and the American Mind* (New Haven, 1967).

19. William E. Unrau, *The Kansa Indians: A History of the Wind People, 1673–1873* (Norman, 1971); George Clarke to Cumming, November 3, 1855, LR-OIA, RG 75, M 234, R 680, F 0150–0151, Potawatomi Agency, NA; McCaslin to Cumming, November 12, 1855, LR-OIA, RG 75, M 234, R 645, F 0070, Osage River Agency, NA; Caleb Smith to Abraham Lincoln, March 5, 1862, President's Messages on Indian Relations, Records of the Senate (hereafter cited as RS), RG 46; S. H. Woodson to Jacob Thompson, June 12, 1855, LR-ID, ID, RG 48, M 825, R 19, F 1049–1050, NA; and

John C. McCoy to Manypenny, October 10, 1855, LR-OIA, RG 75, M 234, R 809, F 0173–0174, Shawnee Agency, NA.

20. "Meeting of the Settlers of the Miami Indian Lands," undesignated newspaper clipping with n.d., LR-OIA, RG 75, M 234, R 646, F 0321, Osage River Agency, NA; *U.S. Statutes at Large*, X (March 3, 1847), 203204; B. A. James to Manypenny, August 8, 1853, LR-OIA, RG 75, M 234, R 733, F 0195, Sac and Fox Agency, NA; William Badger to A. B. Greenwood, February 7, 1860, LR-OIA, RG 75, M 234, R 371, F 0384–0386, Kickapoo Agency, NA; Clarke to Cumming, June 19, 1856, LR-OIA, RG 75, M 234, R 680, F 0136, Potawatomi Agency, NA; and *Kansas Weekly Herald*, July 31, 1858.

21. Andreas, *History of the State of Kansas*, 86, 100–101, 104–105.

22. Frank H. Hodder, "The Railroad Background of the Kansas-Nebraska Bill," *Mississippi Valley Historical Review*, XII (June, 1925), 3–22; Malin, *Nebraska Question*; Nichols, *Disruption of American Democracy*; Gates, *Fifty Million Acres*; *National Intelligencer*, August 9, 1855; *Kansas Weekly Herald*, December 22, 1854, August 26, 1855; Manypenny to McClelland, January 12, 1853, GIC-ID, ID, RG 48, Box 4, NA; McClelland to President of the United States, July 26, 1855, SCLS-ID, ID, RG 48, M 606, R 2, F 0135, NA; R. H. and C. Miller to Cumming, November 5, 1855, LR-OIA, RG 75, M 234, R 809, F 0108–0109, Shawnee Agency, NA; Reeder to Franklin Pierce, February 27, 1855, George Clarke to A. B. Greenwood, December 12, 1856, LR-OIA, RG 75, M 234, R 680, 681, F 0193–0194, 0346–0347, Potawatomi Agency, NA.

23. Reeder to Manypenny, March 30, 1855, LR-OIA, RG 75, M 234, R 452, F 0710–0716, Miscellaneous Letters, NA.

24. *National Intelligencer*, May 15, 25, 1855.

25. *Ibid.*, August 9, 1855; Manypenny to George Whiting, October 14, 1856, GIC-ID, ID, RG 48, Box 5, NA; Charles Mix to Jacob Thompson, December 9, 1857, GIC-ID, ID, RG 48, Box 6, NA; Job Samuel to Commissioner of Indian Affairs, December 14, 1858, LR-OIA, RG 75, M 234, R 275, F 0022, Delaware Agency, NA; and Andreas, *History of the State of Kansas*, 100–101, 104–105.

CHAPTER TWO: THE CAPITALIZATION OF NATURE

1. Marx, *Machine in the Garden;* David Emmons, *Garden in the Grasslands: Boomer Literature of the Central Great Plains* (Lincoln, 1971); Baldwin Möllhausen, *Dairy of a Journey from the Mississippi to the Coast of the Pacific,* 2 vols. (London, 1858); James W. Hurst, *Law and Economic Growth in the Legal History of the Timber Industry in Wisconsin* (Cambridge, 1964); and Robert McCloskey, *American Conservatism in the Age of Enterprise: A Study of William Graham Sumner, Stephen J. Field and Andrew Carnegie* (Cambridge, 1951).

2. Kappler, *Treaties,* II, 614–626, 631–646, 800–803, 878–881, 942–950.

3. *Ibid.,* 803–807, 814–828, 835–839.

4. *Ibid.,* 824–828, 835–839, 803–807.

5. H. Craig Miner, *The Corporation and the Indian: Tribal Sovereignty and Industrial Civilization in Indian Territory* (Columbia, Mo., 1976); *Senate Executive Document No. 51,* 50th Cong., 1st Sess., III, Pt. 4 (Serial 2506), 1595, 1673–1675.

6. Kappler, *Treaties,* II, 614–618; David G. Taylor, "Boom Town Leavenworth: The Failure of a Dream," *Kansas Historical Quarterly,* XXXVIII, No. 4 (Winter, 1972), 407–408; Thomas Sykes to A. B. Greenwood, May 30, 1860, File 36B-C5, RS, RG 46, NA; *Kansas State Record* (Topeka), July 14, 1860; M. Howard Irwin to President, August 11, 1865, LR-ID, ID, RG 48, M 825, NA; and Gates, *Fifty Million Acres,* 120. C. A. Weslager, *The Delaware Indians* (New Brunswick, 1972), 414, finds one Indian charge that the chiefs who signed the 1860 treaty were drunk. However, Weslager's account of this tribe in Kansas is brief and consists mainly of an analysis of the treaties.

7. T. Sykes to House Committee on Indian Affairs, February 1, 1861, Package 37A-E7.4, RHR, RG 233, NA.

8. J. C. Douglas to M. F. Conway, June 17, 1861, LR-OIA, RG 75, M 234, R 4, F 0050, Sac and Fox Agency, NA; P. C. Ferguson to Lyman Trumball, March 22, 1862, LR-OIA, RG 75, M 234, R 276, F 0259, Delaware Agency, NA.

9. Caleb Smith to E. M. Stanton, April 14, 1862, SCLS-ID, ID, RG 48, M 606, R 4, F 0050, NA; J. B. Reynolds to C. B. Smith, July 7, 1862, LR-OIA, RG 75, M 234, R 276, F 0234, Delaware Agency, NA; T. Johnson to H. B. Branch, October

6, 1862, *ibid.*, F 0051; and John Quick to [Secretary of the Interior], August 18, 1863, LR-ID, ID, RG 48, M 825, R 21, F 0397, NA.

10. F. Johnson to H. B. Branch, May 16, 1862, LR-OIA, RG 75, M 234, R 276, F 0411, Delaware Agency, NA; F. Johnson to William Dole, December 10, 1863, GIC-ID, ID, RG 48, Box 12, NA; John Conner, Charles Journeycake *et al.* to Commissioner of Indian Affairs, August 5, 1862, LR-OIA, RG 75, M 234, R 276, F 0087, Delaware Agency, NA; and R. W. Thompson to William Dole, December 16, 1864, *ibid.*, F 1239–1240.

11. James Harlan to John Furent, October 13, 1865, SCLS-ID, ID, RG 48, M 606, R 5, F 0253, NA; W. H. Widener to W. H. Seward, November LR-ID, ID, RG 48, Box 15, NA; J. H. Lane to Harlan, December 14, 1865, LR-ID, ID, RG 48, M 825, R 22, F 1257–1258, NA; and Thomas Murphy to Harlan, December 22, 1865, GIC-ID, ID, "Delaware Lands, Sale to Missouri River R. R. Co.," Special File 91, RG 48, NA.

12. H. Bartling to D. N. Cooley, April 5, 1866, LR-OIA, RG 75, M 234, R 277, F 0713–0714, Delaware Agency, NA; H. Bartling to Cooley, September 10, 1866, GIC-ID, ID, "Delaware Lands, Sale to Missouri River R. R. Co.," Special File 91, RG 48, NA; Bartling to Thomas Murphy, October 1, 1866, *ibid.*; and James Harlan to "Gentlemen," August 16, 1865, SCLS-ID, ID, RG 48, M 606, R 5, F 0201–0205, NA.

13. O. W. Holmes, *The Common Law* (Boston, 1881); and Gates, *Fifty Million Acres,* 107.

14. Kappler, *Treaties,* II, 937–938; Gates, *Fifty Million Acres,* 116–123; and Elmo Richardson and Alan Farley, *John Palmer Usher: Lincoln's Secretary of the Interior* (Lawrence, 1960), 15, 33, 51, 53, 60–61.

15. Kappler, *Treaties,* II, 937–938.

16. Thomas Murphy to D. N. Cooley, October 1, 1866, LR-OIA, RG 75, M 234, R 277, F 0846–0847, Delaware Agency, NA; W. H. Watson to Cooley, July 14, RG 46, 1866, RS, File 39B-C6, NA; and J. P. Usher to O. H. Browning, October 9, 1866, LR-ID, ID, RG 48, M 606, R 23, F 0577–0590, NA.

17. Thomas Murphy to R. B. Van Vankenburg, September 5, 1865, LR-OIA, RG 75, M 234, R 277, F 0189–0190, Delaware Agency, NA; H. Bartling to Murphy, September 18, 1866,

GIC-ID, ID, Special File 91, RG 48, NA; and Murphy to O. H. Browning, May 2, 1867, LR-ID, ID, RG 48, M 825, R 23, F 0939–0941, NA.

18. Gates, *Fifty Million Acres*, 131.

19. John Perry to D. N. Cooley, December 11, 1865, LR-OIA, RG 75, M 234, R 685, F 0370, Potawatomi Agency, NA; J. P. Usher to O. H. Browning, October 3, 1866, *ibid.*, F 0116–0117; J. W. Headley to Browning, October 10, 1866, GIC-ID, ID, Box 768, Special File 97, "Potawatomi Trust Lands," RG 48, NA; Usher to Browning, October 20, 1866, *ibid.;* Usher to Lewis Bogy, November 9, 1866, LR-OIA, RG 75, M 234, R 687, F 0126–0128, Potawatomi Agency, NA; W. T. Otto to C. E. Mix, September 19, 1867, *ibid.*, R 686, F 0064–0065; and Kappler, *Treaties*, II 824–828.

20. Gates, *Fifty Million Acres*, 143–144; and J. P. Usher to J. H. Lane, February 25, 1865, SCLS-ID, ID, RG 48, M 606, R 5, F 0099, NA.

21. A. M. Gibson, *The Kickapoos: Lords of the Middle Border* (Norman, 1963), 124; R. Baldwin to J. Hawley, December 4, 1857, LR-OIA, RG 75, M 234, R 371, F 0171–0172, Kickapoo Agency, NA; Benjamin Holladay to C. E. Mix, April 15, 1869, *ibid.*, F 0328; W. P. Badger to A. M. Robinson, February 17, 1859, *ibid.*, F 0329; Badger to Robinson, May 16, 1859, *ibid.*, F 0350–0354; James Price to Robinson, July 26, 1859, *ibid.*, F 0357–0359; and Badger to A. B. Greenwood, February 2, 1860, *ibid.*, F 0378–0379.

22. Gates, *Fifty Million Acres*, 136–137.

23. Caleb Smith to William Dole, May 20, 1862, SCLS-ID, ID, RG 48, M 606, R 4, F 0061; and "Testimony in Dole Investigation," May 5, 1863, LR-OIA, RG 75, M 234, R 372, F 0162–0177, Kickapoo Agency, NA.

24. Testimony before W. W. Guthrie, June 8, 1863, LR-OIA, RG 75, M 234, R 371, F 0634–0636, Kickapoo Agency, NA; Albert Horton to Samuel Pomeroy, *ibid.*, F 0753–0754; C. B. Keith to Pomeroy, June 20, 1863, *ibid.*, F 0756–0757; J. H. Lane to J. P. Usher, September 15, 1863, LR-ID, ID, RG 48, M 825, R 21, F 0427–0428, NA; W. W. Guthrie, Brief, n.d., LR-OIA, RG 75, M 234, R 372, F 0221–0227, Kickapoo Agency, NA; and Charles Keith to Dole, *ibid.*, F 0727–0732.

25. Gates, *Fifty Million Acres*, 138–139.

26. F. G. Adams to Thomas Murphy, February 3, 1866, LR-OIA,

RG 75, M 234, R 372, F 0971–0979, Kickapoo Agency, NA; Murphy to D. N. Cooley, February 27, 1866, *ibid.;* and S. C. Pomeroy to James Harlan, June 30, 1866, LR-ID, ID, RG 48, R 23, F 0471, NA.

27. Winthrop Jordan, *White Over Black: American Attitudes Toward the Negro, 1550–1812* (Chapel Hill, 1968); and Stanley Elkins, *Slavery: A Problem in American Institutional and Intellectual Life* (Chicago, 1959).

28. Samuel Cormatzter to J. Thompson, July 8, 1858, LR-OIA, RG 75, M 234, R 810, F 0013–0014, Shawnee Agency, NA; and Benjamin Newsom to A. M. Robinson, September 2, 1858, *ibid.,* F 0128–0131.

29. R. S. Stevens to C. E. Mix, August 20, 1860, LR-OIA, RG 75, M 234, R 737, F 0514, Sac and Fox Agency; C. C. Hutchinson to William Dole, May 24, 1861, *ibid.;* F. 0675–0676; John Burbank to H. B. Branch, January 4, 1862, LR-OIA, RG 75, M 234, R 309, F 0889, Great Nemaha Agency, NA; Thomas Murphy to D. N. Cooley, July 17, 1866, LR-OIA, RG 75, M 234, R 686, F 0251, Potawatomi Agency, NA; and George Manypenny to Robert McClelland, January 9, 1856, GIC-ID, ID, RG 48, Box 4, NA.

30. Thomas Le Duc, "History and Appraisal of U.S. Land Policy in 1862," in Allan Bogue, Thomas Phillips and James Wrights, eds., *The West of the American People* (Itasca, Illinois, 1970), 206–207.

31. Andrew Dorn to C. E. Mix, January 18, 1858, LR-OIA, RG 75, M 234, R 531, F 0059, Neosho Agency, NA; and Martin to D. N. Cooley, May 21, 1866, LR-OIA, RG 75, M 234, R 736, F 0380, Sac and Fox Agency, NA.

CHAPTER THREE: THE INDIAN RING

1. *Congressional Globe,* 33d Cong., 2d Sess., XXIV (February 12, 1855), 684, 703; *ibid.,* 38th Cong., 2d Sess., XXV (March 12, 1865), 1299; James Blunt to J. P. Usher, August 1, 1863, LR-ID, ID, RG 48, M 825, R 21, F 0371–0372; and *Leavenworth Daily Conservative* (Leavenworth, Kansas), October 29, 1867.

2. *Leavenworth Daily Conservative,* July 19, October 8, 1867; and *Annual Report of the Commissioner of Indian Affairs,* 1855, 97, 100.

3. William E. Unrau, "The Civilian as Indian Agent: Villain

or Victim?", *The Western Historical Quarterly*, III (October, 1972), 405–420; Alexander Cumming to George Manypenny, June 15, 1856, November 28, 1856, LR-OIA, RG 75, M 234, R 809, F 0245, 0287–0288, Shawnee Agency, NA; George Clarke to Cumming, December 5, 1856, LR-OIA, RG 75, M 234, R 680, F 0351–0352, NA; Unrau, *The Kansa Indians*, 174–175; Charles Mix to W. T. Otto, September 19, 1867, GIC-ID, ID, RG 48, Box 19, NA; and G. C. Snow to N. G. Taylor, April 13, 1867, Old Neosho Agency Records, Box 415040, Federal Records Center, Fort Worth, Texas.

4. G. C. Snow to Charles Mix, October 16, 1867, LR-OIA, RG 75, M 234, R 534, F 0797, NA; and N. G. Taylor to O. H. Browning, November 18, 1868, GIC-ID, ID, RG 48, Box 22, NA.

5. *The Kansas Chief* (White Cloud, Kansas), December 21, 1867.

6. *In the Supreme Court of the State of Kansas* (January Term, 1860). *Albert Wiley, Plaintiff vs. Keokuk, Chief of the Sac and Fox Indians, Defendant on Petition in Error. Argument and Brief for the Defendant By James Christian*, LR-OIA, RG 75, M 234, R 738, F 0525, Sac and Fox Agency, NA; George Powers, to Commissioner of Indian Affairs, August 12, 1870, *ibid.*, F 0637; and Perry Fuller to President of the United States, February 14, 1867, *ibid.*, R 737, F 0071, NA.

7. George Ewing to Owen Connally, April 29, 1853, LR-OIA, RG 75, M 234, R 733, F 0167, Sac and Fox Agency, NA; Thomas Connally to ?, March 24, 1853, *ibid.*, F 0171–0172; Keokuk and others to Governor John Geary, March 17, 1857, *ibid.*, F 0626–0628; J. Thompson to C. E. Mix, April 6, 1859, SCLS-ID, ID, RG 48, M 606, R 3, F 0131, NA; W. R. Irwin to D. N. Cooley, October 9, 1866, LR-OIA, RG 75, M 234, R 736, F 0296–0303, Sac and Fox Agency, NA; Mo-ko-ho-ko to Commissioner of Indian Affairs, n.d., *ibid.*, R 737, F 0082 ff.; and A. Gokey to Commissioner of Indian Affairs, April 10, 1866, *ibid.* An excellent aid in the identification of the various Indian agents and their terms of office is Edward E. Hill, *The Office of Indian Affairs, 1824–1880: Historical Sketches* (New York, 1974).

8. F. Tymany to C. Mix, November 4, June 13, April 11, 1858, LR-OIA, RG 75, M 234, R 733, F 0715–0719, 0690, 0694, Sac and Fox Agency, NA; and Ida M. Ferris, "The Sacs and

Foxes in Franklin and Osage Counties, Kansas," *Collections of the Kansas State Historical Society,* XI (1910), 352.

9. F. Tymany to C. E. Mix, April 11, 1858, LR-OIA, RG 75, M 234, R 733, F 0674, Sac and Fox Agency, NA; and Tymany to James W. Denver, February 28, 1859, *ibid.,* R 734, F 0056–0058.

10. Francis McCoons to A. M. Robinson, December 11, 1859, *ibid.,* R 734, F 0276; Keokuk to D. N. Cooley, April 22, 1866, *ibid.,* R 736, F 0371–0372; and O. H. Browning to Commissioner of Indian Affairs, November 16, 1868, SCLS-ID, ID, RG 48, M 606, R 9, F 0151, NA.

11. John Conner to Abraham Lincoln, December 20, 1862, LR-OIA, RG 75, M 234, R 276, F 0217, Delaware Agency, NA; Wyandot Chiefs to William Dole, March 29, 1863, *ibid.,* F 0832; and Samuel C. Pomeroy to C. B. Smith, July 19, 1861, GIC-ID, ID, RG 48, Box 9, NA.

12. F. Johnson to William Dole, January 15, 1863, LR-OIA, RG 75, M 234, R 276, F 0517, Delaware Agency, NA; and William Clough to To Whom It May Concern, January 7, 1863, *ibid.,* F 0526–0528.

13. M. M. Marberry, *The Golden Voice: A Biography of Isaac Kalloch* (New York, 1947), 165–166; John T. Jones to William Dole, April 26, 1861, C. C. Hutchinson to Dole, April 30, 1861, Hutchinson to H. B. Branch, July 10, September 20, 1861, Undated Receipt (1861?), three Sac and Fox chiefs to Dole, September 10, 1861, John P. Usher to Dole, October 16, 1861, Branch to Dole, November 20, 1861, LR-OIA, RG 75, M 234, R 734, *passim,* Sac and Fox Agency, NA; various letters between C. C. Hutchinson and the Indian Office in Washington, 1862–1864, LR-OIA, RG 75, M 234, R 655–656, *passim,* Ottawa Agency, NA; Special File 95, Special Files, ID, ID, RG 48, *passim,* NA; and Special Cases of Office of Indian Affairs, RG 75, Special Case No. 126, "Ottawa University," *passim,* NA.

14. Kat-he-cut-te-da-da *et al.,* to James Harlan, August 12, 1865, LR-ID, ID, RG 48, M 825, R 22, F 0875–0856; and James Abbott to Commissioner of Indian Affairs, March 11, 1865, LR-OIA, RG 75, M 234, R 0813, F 0321–0322, Shawnee Agency, NA.

15. G. B. Mitchell to D. J. Morrill, July 25, 1870, LR-ID, ID,

RG 48, M 825, R 25, F 1030, NA; and Edward Earle to C. Delano, January 16, 1872, *ibid.*, R 27, F 0036–0037.

16. William Dole to J. P. Usher, January 21, 1863, GIC-ID, ID, RG 48, Box 11, NA; and Perry Fuller to A. B. Greenwood, October 19, 1859, LR-OIA, RG 75, M 234, R 734, F 0160, Sac and Fox Agency, NA.

17. George Ewing to George Manypenny, January 5, 1854, LR-OIA, RG 75, M 234, R 451, F 0311–0316, Miscellaneous, NA.

18. John Goodell to George Manypenny, April 11, 1854, LR-OIA, RG 75, M 234, R 733, F 0312, Sac and Fox Agency, NA; George Clarke to Alexander Cumming, June 14, 1855, LR-OIA, RG 75, M 234, R 680, F 0044, Potawatomi Agency, NA; and Jude Bourassa and Pategoshuc to Manypenny, September 17, 1855, *ibid.*, F 0011.

19. *Annual Report of the Commissioner of Indian Affairs*, 1855, 288 ff.

20. Statement, September, 1955, LR-OIA, RG 75, M 234, R 809, F 0068–0081, Shawnee Agency, NA.

21. *Ibid.;* R. W. McClelland to Commissioner of Indian Affairs, December 28, 1855, *ibid.*, F 0160; A. J. Isaacs to F. Pierce, November 8, 1856, *ibid.*, F 0344–0345; Manypenny to R. McClelland, November 14, 1856, *ibid.*, F 0730–0740; and R. W. Thompson to Jacob Thompson, December 9, 1857, LR-ID, ID, RG 48, M 825, R 19, F 0577–0582, NA.

22. Junnis Hillyer to Howell Cobb, January 12, 1858, LR-ID, ID, RG 48, M 825, R 19, F 0620–0621; C. Mix to J. Thompson, June 16, 1858, GIC-ID, ID, RG 48, Box 6, NA; and C. F. Barnes to Junnis Hillyer, April 24, 1858, LR-ID, ID, RG 48, M 825, R 19, F 0931–0932, NA.

23. *New York Times*, December 20, 1868; and *Senate Report No. 4240* (February 2, 1905), 58th Cong., 3d Sess. (Serial 4756).

24. James Abbott and Matthew King testimony, January, 1862, LR-OIA, RG 75, M 234, R 812, F 0404–3126, Shawnee Agency, NA.

25. *Ibid.;* William Dole to C. B. Smith, December 26, 1861, GIC-ID ID, RG 48, Box 10, NA.

26. James W. Denver to Robert Stevens, May 15, 1857, "Papers Concerning Trust Lands of Peorias," RG 48, Special File 96, Box 768, NA; Denver to Stevens, May 19, 1857, *ibid.;* and Stevens to Denver, October 13, 1857, *ibid.*

27. Confederated Peorias, etc., to Commissioner of Indian Affairs, May 16, 1863, LR-OIA, RG 75, M 234, F 0056, Osage River Agency, NA.

28. Kappler, *Indian Treaties*, II, 796–803; Contract, September 22, 1859, LR-OIA, RG 75, M 234, R 737, F 0110, Sac and Fox Agency, NA; *Senate Report No. 4240* (February 2, 1905), 58th Cong., 3d Sess. (Serial 4756), 114 ff.; and Perry Fuller to A. B. Greenwood, December 7, 1860, LR-OIA, RG 75, M 234, R 734, F 0225, Sac and Fox Agency, NA.

29. *Senate Report No. 4240* (February 2, 1905), 58th Cong., 3d Sess. (Serial 4756), 114 ff.; Keokuk and others to C. C. Hutchinson, November 29, 1861, LR-OIA, RG 75, M 234, R 734, F 0705–0706, Sac and Fox Agency, NA; Caleb Smith to James R. Doolittle, November 27, 1862, SCLS-ID, ID, RG 48, M 606, R 4, F 0064; J. P. Usher to Charles Mix, August 22, 1862, *ibid.*, F 0087; William Dole to C. B. Smith, November 15, 1862, GIC-ID, ID, RG 48 Box 11, NA; R. McBratney to J. P. Usher, March 9, 1863, LR-ID, ID, RG 48, M 825, R 21, F 0119, NA; R. S. Stevens to Usher, March 10, 1863, *ibid.*, F 0123–0124; Stevens to A. B. Greenwood, May 8, 1860, LR-OIA, RG 75, M 234, R 811, F 0455–0456, Shawnee Agency, NA; and *Vinita Chieftain*, April 23, 1885.

30. R. S. Stevens to J. P. Usher, January 4, 1865, LR-ID, ID, RG 48, M 825, R 22, F 0005–0006, NA; F. W. Holland to James Harlan, December 18, 1866, GIC-ID, ID, RG 48, Box 17, NA; Horatio Woodman to Secretary of the Interior, January 7, 1868, LR-ID, ID, RG 48, M 825, R 24, F 0321–0322, NA; and Charles Mix to O. H. Browning, January 14, 1868, GIC-ID, ID, RG 48, Box 19, NA.

31. Edward Clark to Charles Mix, September 7, 1860, LR-OIA, RG 75, M 234, R 811, F 0134, Shawnee Agency, NA; Certificate showing Stevens' purchases, 1867, RG 48, Special File 98, Box 768, NA; Jesse Morrin to Commissioner of Indian Affairs, August 9, 1859, LR-OIA, RG 75, M 234, R 532, F 0094–0095, Neosho Agency, NA; and Charles Mix to Fielding Johnson, August 11, 1862, GIC-ID, ID, RG 48, Box 10, NA.

CHAPTER FOUR: THE GOVERNMENT CHIEF

1. Vine Deloria, Jr., *Custer Died for Your Sins: An Indian Manifesto* (New York, 1970), 203.

2. Kappler, *Treaties*, II, 353–356, 367–370, 372–375, 557–560; three principal chiefs, fourteen counselors, and seven braves to Superintendent of Indian Affairs, April 2, 1858, LR-OIA, RG 75, M 234, R 681, F 0223–0224, Potawatomi Agency, NA.

3. W. E. Murphy to John Haverly, November 24, 1857, and Murphy to Council of Potawatomies, April 19, 1858, LR-OIA, RG 75, M 234, R 681, F 0058, 0207–0208, Potawatomi Agency, NA; *Kansas Weekly Herald* (Leavenworth), March 21, 1857.

4. Murphy to John Haverly, November 24, 1857, LR-OIA, RG 75, M 234, R 681, F 0058, Potawatomi Agency, NA; Murphy to A. M. Robinson, August 23, 1859, *ibid.*, R 682, F 0123–0124.

5. Joseph Murphy, "Potawatomies of the West: Origins of the Citizens Band" (unpublished Ph.D. dissertation, History Department, University of Oklahoma, 1961), 371–372.

6. Kappler, *Treaties*, II, 824–825; Gates, *Fifty Million Acres*, 128–129; William Ross to Commissioner of Indian Affairs, March 17, 1863, LR-OIA, RG 75, M 234, R 683, F 0128, Potawatomi Agency, NA; Edward Wolcott to William Dole, February 14, 1865, *ibid.*, R 685, F 0139.

7. Andreas, *History of the State of Kansas*, 159, 178; Gates, *Fifty Million Acres*, 128; Ross to Commissioner of Indian Affairs, March 10, 1862, LR-OIA, RG 75, M 234, R 683, F 0368, Potawatomi; Palmer to Thomas Murphy, November 20, 1866, *ibid.*, R 687, F 0351–0352.

8. Ross to William Dole, July 8, 1862, LR-OIA, RG 75, M 234, R 683, F 0426, Potawatomi Agency, NA; Luther Palmer to D. N. Cooley, April 5, 1866, *ibid.*, R. 687, F 0394; Palmer to Thomas Murphy, January 1, 1868, *ibid.*, R 688, F 0219–0221; Bourassa, Navarre, Bertrand, and several other "delegates" of the Potawatomi Nation to Palmer, March 12, 1868, *ibid.*, F 0020; Palmer to N. G. Taylor, March 12, 1868, *ibid.*, F 0021.

9. Kappler, *Treaties*, II, 916; Ross to Commissioner of Indian Affairs, March 17, 1863, LR-OIA, RG 75, M 234, R 684, F 0128, Potawatomi Agency, NA; Bourassa, Navarre, and Bertrand to D. N. Cooley, March 12, 1866, *ibid.*, R 687, F 0282; Luther Palmer to Lewis Bogy, February 11, 1867, *ibid.*, R 686, F 0298–0299.

10. Murphy to Taylor, July 18, 1867, LR-OIA, RG 75, M 234, R 686, F 0205, Potawatomi Agency, NA; Alexander Bushman to Taylor, October 23, 1868, *ibid.*, F 0035–0036; Bushman to Ely Parker, March 11, 1870, *ibid.*, R 690, F 0090–0100; Hill, *The Office of Indian Affairs*, 141.

11. Joel Morris to Enoch Hoag, December 12, 1869, LR-OIA, RG 75, M 234, R 689, F 0100, NA; Kappler, *Treaties*, II, 974.

12. Morris to Hoag, June 5, August 22, 1870, Potawatomi Agency Miscellaneous Correspondence, Book 1, Federal Records Center, Kansas City.

13. Ruth Landes, *The Prairie Potawatomi* (Madison, 1970), 13; Gates, *Fifty Million Acres*, 145–146.

14. Gates, *Fifty Million Acres*, 146; Kappler, *Treaties*, II, 618–623.

15. Edward Clark to Charles Mix, January 5, September 19, 1859, LR-OIA, RG 75, M 234, R 810, F 0021–0023, 1208–1215, Shawnee Agency, NA; W. G. Melville and others to President James Buchanan, n.d., 1860, and Paschal Fish *et al.* to Commissioner of Indian Affairs, February 6, 1860, *ibid.*, R 811, F 0478, 0076–0079.

16. Andreas, *History of the State of Kansas*, 624–625; Kappler, *Treaties*, II, 623.

17. B. J. Newsom to A. M. Robinson, April 5 and 17, 1860, LR-OIA, RG 75, M 234, R 811, F 0344–0345, Shawnee Agency, NA.

18. Abelard Guthrie to Commissioner of Indian Affairs, December 26, 1865, LR-OIA, RG 75, M 234, R 814, F 0878–0879, Shawnee Agency, NA; Graham Rogers *et al.* to Indian Committee in Congress, November 19, 1866, *ibid.*, R 815, F 0295–0300; Lewis Bogy to O. H. Browning, March 2, 1867, RS, RG 46, 40B C7, NA; "The Shawnee Indians," Prepared by Abelard Guthrie of Kansas, March 23, 1868, RG 75, Special Case 128, "Black Bob Shawnee," NA, 10–11; Gates, *Fifty Million Acres*, 38–39.

19. Kappler, *Treaties*, II, 835–839; "Testimony in Dole Investigation," May 5, 1863, LR-OIA, RG 75, M 234, R 372, F 0162–0177, Kickapoo Agency, NA; Gates, *Fifty Million Acres*, 136–139; Gibson, *The Kickapoos*, 133–135.

20. Gibson, *The Kickapoos*, 131–136; Hill, *The Office of Indian Affairs*, 85; Murphy to D. N. Cooley, September 11, 1866,

LR-OIA, RG 75, M 234, R 372, F 1109–1115, Kickapoo Agency, NA.

21. Kappler, *Treaties*, II, 838; Gibson, *The Kickapoos*, 136–138; Gates, *Fifty Million Acres*, 198–199.

22. H. B. Branch to Charles Mix, February 28, 1862; John Conner and other Delaware delegates to William P. Dole, June 3, 1862, LR-OIA, RG 75, M 234, R 276, F 0013, 0083, Delaware Agency, NA; George C. Snow to W. Byers, December 29, 1866, Old Neosho Agency Correspondence, Box 415040, Federal Records Center, Fort Worth, Texas.

23. J. B. Chapman to Charles Mix, October 28, 1867, LR-OIA, RG 75, M 234, R 534, F 0391, Neosho Agency, NA.

24. William Woodman to William G. Coffin, April 1, 1863, *ibid.*, R 533, F 0229; John Pratt to William P. Dole, December 23, 1864, LR-OIA, RG 75, M 234, R 277, F 0007, Delaware Agency, NA; R. Brackenridge to Secretary of the Interior, July 5, 1865, LR-ID, ID, RG 48, M 825, R 22, F 0079, NA; Statement of John Wilson, William Hurr, and James Wind, April 15, 1869, RG 75, Special Case 126, "Ottawa University," NA; John T. Jones to President U. S. Grant, April 29, 1869, and Wilson, Hurr, Wind, and thirteen Ottawa leaders to Commissioner of Indian Affairs, May 10, 1869, LR-OIA, RG 75, M234, R 657, F 0412, Ottawa Agency, NA.

25. P. Richard Metcalf, "Who Should Rule at Home? Native American Politics and Indian-White Relations," *The Journal of American History*, XLI (December, 1974), 651–653. See also Robert F. Berkhofer, Jr., "The Political Context of a New Indian History," *Pacific Historical Review*, XL (August, 1971), 357–382.

26. Unrau, *The Kansa Indians*, 50, 118–119.

27. Kappler, *Treaties*, II, 552–554; Unrau, *The Kansa Indians*, 161–194, 214–215; William E. Unrau, *The Kaw People* (Phoenix, 1975), 66–76.

28. Three chiefs, fourteen counselors, and seven braves of the Potawatomi Nation to Superintendent of Indian Affairs, April 2, 1858, LR-OIA, RG 75, M 234, R 681, F 0223–0224, Potawatomi Agency, NA; Lewis Bogy to O. H. Browning, February 27, 1867, RS, RG 46, 40B C5, NA; Landes, *The Prairie Potawatomi*, 13; J. B. Chapman to Charles Mix, October 28, 1867, LR-OIA, RG 75, M 234, R 534, F 0391,

Neosho Agency, NA; Metcalf, "Who Shall Rule at Home?",
654–657, 661–665.

29. Metcalf, "Who Shall Rule at Home?", 657–661; William T.
Hagan, *The Sac and Fox Indians* (Norman, 1958), 233;
Kappler, *Treaties,* II, 613–633.

30. B. A. James to George Manypenny, May 4, 1854, LR-OIA,
RG 75, M 234, R 733, F 0282, Sac and Fox Agency, NA;
Daniel Vanderslice to Alexander Cumming, December 30,
1854 and November 3, 1855, LR-OIA, RG 75, M 234, R 308,
F 0559, 0719, Great Nemaha Agency, NA; Vanderslice to
Cumming, March 31, 1857, *ibid.,* R 309, F 0112; Pet-te-oke-
o-mah and twelve Missouri Sac and Fox leaders to Com-
missioner of Indian Affairs, interpreted by Frank Goken,
December 27, 1857, *ibid.,* F 0637; "Interview" between
Ne-sour-quoit and Charles Mix, January 20, 1858, *ibid.,*
F 0654–0677; Notes of the speeches of the principal chief
and other of the Sac and Foxes of Missouri in council held
at the Great Nemaha Agency, April 26, 1859, *ibid.,* F 1031–
1035.

31. Talk, Perry Fuller to Keokuk, June 22, 1859, LR-OIA, RG
75, M 234, R 734, F 0083–0088, Sac and Fox Agency, NA;
Fuller to A. B. Greenwood, July 4, 1859, *ibid.,* F 0096–0097;
Francis McKonce to Commissioner of Indian Affairs, n.d.,
1865, *ibid.,* R 736, F 0008; B. A. Martin to D. N. Cooley,
May 18, 1866, *ibid.,* F 0385; *Kansas Weekly Herald* (Lawrence), October 15, 1859.

32. Hiram W. Farnsworth to Lewis Bogy, February n.d., 1867,
and James Chipman to President of the United States, February 23, 1867, LR-OIA, RG 75, M 234, R 737, F 0033, Sac
and Fox Agency, NA; Keokuk to Secretary of the Interior,
January 9, 1968, and Thomas Murphy to N. G. Taylor,
February 8, 1869, *ibid.,* R 738, F 0187, 0215.

33. Enoch Hoag to E. S. Parker, December 1, 1869, *ibid.,* F
0587; H. C. Linn to E. A. Hayt, Potawatomi Agency Miscellaneous Correspondence, Book 6, Federal Records Center,
Kansas City; Hagan, *Sac and Fox Indians,* 243.

CHAPTER FIVE: THE CLAIM OF THE SOIL

1. *Smoky Hill and Republican Union* (Junction City), January
31, February 14, 1863; *National Intelligencer,* June 9, 1855;
Wabaunsee County Herald, June 3, 1869.

2. Taylor, "Boom Town Leavenworth," 392–393, 395–396.
3. George Manypenny to Robert McClelland, September 26, 1862, LR-ID, ID, RG 48, M 825, R 19, F 0839; *Kansas Weekly Herald*, September 15, September 22, 1854; *National Intelligencer*, November 7, 1854, March 3, 1855.
4. Manypenny to Secretary of Interior, January 20, 1855, GIC-ID, ID, RG 48, Box 4, NA; *Kansas Weekly Herald*, March 8, 1856, October 20, 1854; Manypenny to McClelland, September 29, 1855, GIC-ID, ID, RG 48, Box 4, NA.
5. Manypenny to McClelland, September 29, 1855, GIC-ID, ID, RG 48, Box 4, NA; McClelland to Jefferson Davis, October 11, 1854, cited in *Senate Executive Document No. 50,* 33d Cong., 2d Sess. (Serial 752), 1; George Clark to A. Cumming, November 13, 1854, LR-OIA, RG 75, M 234, R 679, F 0620, Potawatomi Agency, NA.
6. *Kansas Weekly Herald,* February 23, March 8, 1856; E. A. Ogden to E. Hudson, November 3, 1854, cited in *Senate Executive Document No. 50,* 33d Cong., 2d Sess. (Serial 752), 15–16; *House Executive Document No. 50,* 33d Cong., 2d Sess. (Serial 783), 42.
7. *Kansas Weekly Herald,* November 22, 29, March 1, 1856; *National Intelligencer,* January 1, 1857; James Rollins to Secretary of Interior, July 22, 1862, LR-OIA, RG 75, M 234, R 276, F 0246, Delaware Agency, NA.
8. *National Intelligencer,* May 12, 1857; Joseph Killbuck, Frederick Samuel to James Buchanan, February 12, 1858, LR-OIA, RG 75, M 234, R 275, F 0095–0096, Delaware Agency, NA; Bourassa to Thomas Murphy, August 26, 1866, GID-ID, ID, RG 48, Box 17, NA.
9. *Annual Report of the Commissioner of Indian Affairs* (1855), 92; William King to George Manypenny, June 29, 1855, LR-OIA, RG 75, M 234, R 531, F 0939–0940, Neosho Agency, NA; W. F. M. Arny to A. B. Greenwood, February 13, 1860, *ibid.,* R 532, F 0255–0256; D. Vanderslice to A. Cumming, July 20, 1855, LR-OIA, RG 75, M 234, R 308, F 0700, Great Nemaha Agency, NA; Vanderslice to Manypenny, February 6, 1857, *ibid.,* R. 309, F 0587; *Annual Report of the Commissioner of Indian Affairs* (1858), 106–107; G. C. Johnston to R. C. Shenck, February 25, 1867, LR-OIA, RG 75, M 234, R 815, F 0202–0203, Shawnee Agency, NA; Albert Wiley to Thomas Murphy, August 3, 1868, LR-OIA, RG 75, M 234,

R. 737, F 0438, Sac and Fox Agency, NA; Murphy to N. G. Taylor, June 23, 1868, GIC-ID, ID, RG 48, Box 21, NA; R. M. Phillips to A. Lincoln, March 5, 1862, LR-ID, ID, RG 48, M 825, R 20, F 0593–0594, NA.

10. H. Craig Miner, "The Border Tier Line: A History of the Missouri River, Fort Scott and Gulf Railroad, 1865–1870" (unpublished M. A. thesis, Wichita State University, 1967), 1–34. Miner's study of the M.R.F.S. & G. makes extensive use of the James F. Joy Papers, Burton Collection, Detroit Public Library.

11. *Ibid.*, 128, 30, 32; Gates, *Fifty Million Acres*, 156.

12. Craig Miner, "Border Frontier: The Missouri River, Fort Scott & Gulf Railroad in the Cherokee Neutral Lands, 1868–1870," *Kansas Historical Quarterly*, XXV (Summer, 1969), 106.

13. *Ibid.*, 107–128; Gates, *Fifty Million Acres*, 184.

14. Thomas Patterson to ?, August 5, 1878, LR-OIA, RG 75, M 234, R 870, document P 706, Union Agency, NA; Greenwood to Charles Blair, March 13, 1860, quoted in *National Intelligencer*, March 17, 1860.

15. Issues of *La Cygne Weekly Journal* (Linn City, Kansas) in July, 1870, document the Miami league. These are found in LR-ID, ID, RG 48, M 825, R 26, F 0112–0129, NA. George Reynolds to L. N. Robinson, July 25, 1860, cited in *Annual Report of the Commissioner of Indian Affairs (1860)*, 418; *Miami Reserve Matters. Statement of John Robideaux, Head Chief of the Miami Indians of Kansas* (Paola, Kansas, 1871), in GIC-ID, ID, RG 48, Box 28, NA; W. R. Samples to Secretary of Interior, 1871, LR-OIA, RG 75, M 234, R 104, F 1310–1313, Cherokee Agency, NA.

16. Gates, *Fifty Million Acres*, 196–200.

17. *Ibid.*, 201–210; *Congressional Globe*, June 5, 1868, 40th Cong., 2d Sess., XXXIX, 2895; *ibid.*, June 18, 1868, 3256; *The Humboldt Union*, October 17, 1868; T. and C. Ewing to J. D. Cox, June 2, 1869, Lands and Railroads Division, Department of Interior, RG 48, Box 110, NA; Sen 40B C14, June 10, 1868, RS, RG 46, NA.

18. Gates, *Fifty Million Acres*, 198; I. T. Abelt to Jas. Craig, January 8, 1870, W. R. to George Crawford, August 18, 1869, Louis Reese to Sidney Clarke, December 14, 1868, B. B. Rockwood to Clarke, January 1, 1870, C. W. Babcock

to Clarke, February 8, 1869, November 29, 1868, ? to Clarke, March 28, 1870, Clarke to S. C. Pomeroy, June 20, 1868, A. A. Stewart to Clarke, December 27, 1869, Sidney Clarke papers, Osage Nation Papers, Miscellaneous, Box 443864, Federal Records Center, Fort Worth, Texas.

19. George Snow to E. Sells, March 6, 1866, LR-OIA, RG 75, M 234, R 534, F 0185, Neosho Agency, NA; George Hoyt, *Kansas and the Osage Swindle* (1868), vol. 1, Indian Pamphlets Collection, Kansas State Historical Society.

20. Gates, *Fifty Million Acres*, 222.

21. *Ibid.*, 210, 212, 158; Joseph Wilson to Commissioner of Indian Affairs, June 4, 1870, Lands and Railroads Division, Department of Interior, RG 48, Box 128, NA.

22. R. M. Bratney to Secretary of Interior, February 14, 1868, GIC-ID, ID, RG 48, M 825, R 24, F 0411–0412, NA.

23. J. M. Walker to R. S. Watson, May 21, 1871, to Levi Parsons, August 21, 1871, to S. O. Thacher, August 22, 1871, to Levi Parsons, August 25, 1871, to J. W. Scott, July 25, 1871, to S. A. Slater, September ?, 1871, to S. O. Thacher, July 26, 1871, to J., August 31, 1871, Leavenworth, Lawrence & Galveston Railroad Papers, Burlington Archives, Newberry Library, Chicago, Ill.

24. Walker to Levi Parsons, November 3, 1871, to Thomas Ewing, November 13, 1871, to A. T. Britton, November 24, 1871, to J. F. Joy, December 4, 1871, *ibid.*

25. William Lawrence, *The Reply of Judge Lawrence to the Opinion of the Assistant Attorney General in the Case of the Ceded Lands* (1872), No. 2838, Frank Phillips Collection, University of Oklahoma Library.

26. William Johnston, *Petition for Review Before the Secretary of the Interior. Settlers on the Osage Purchase in Kansas vs. Railroad Companies. Argument for Petitioners by William Johnston of Cincinnati Bar* (Washington, 1870).

27. L. J. Worden to Sidney Clarke, March 20, 1870, ? to Clarke, May 15, 1870, Clarke Papers, Federal Records Center, Fort Worth; C. S. Copeland in *Topeka Capital*, vol. 5, Indian Pamphlets Collection, Kansas State Historical Society; J. M. Walker to S. O. Thacher, February 17, 1872, Leavenworth, Lawrence & Galveston Railroad Papers, Burlington Archives, Newberry Library, Chicago, Illinois. For a comprehensive

account of the situation on the Kaw lands, see Unrau, *The Kansa Indians*, 195–215.

28. S. O. Thacher, *Reply to Briefs of Counsel for Complainant* . . . (n.d.), vol. 5, Indian Pamphlets Collection, Kansas State Historical Society. See also *The United States of America against The Leavenworth, Lawrence & Galveston R.R. Co. and the Missouri, Kansas & Texas R.R. Co.,* vol. 8, *ibid.*

29. Thacher, *Brief.* T. C. Sears, *Brief. The Missouri, Kansas & Texas Railway Co. against Isaac Elidge* (n.d.), vol. 6, Indian Pamphlets Collection, Kansas State Historical Society.

30. George Crawford to James Joy, May 10, 1869, George Crawford Papers, Ablah Library, Wichita State University.

CHAPTER SIX: AND THEN THERE WERE NONE

1. *Ottawa Journal* (Ottawa, Kansas), April 21, 1870; *Sedalia Weekly Democrat,* November 20, 1873; J. H. Morris to Enoch Hoag, August 22, 1870, Letters Sent, Potawatomi Agency, Federal Records Center, Kansas City; *Junction City Western Union,* December 29, 1866; Statement of John Jumper, 1874, Letters Received, Board of Indian Commissioners, RG 75, NA; Kickapoo talk, May 20, 1870, GIC-ID, ID, Box 25, NA.

2. G. C. Snow to Charles Mix, September 9, 1867, Osage Administration Miscellaneous Records, Box 415040, Federal Records Center, Fort Worth; Schedule of Indian Trust Lands in Kansas, January, 1864, HR 40A-F 23.4, RHR, RG 233, NA; Lewis Bogy to House Committee on Indian Affairs, December 13, 1866, HR 39A-F 11.8, *ibid.;* "Instructions to Commissioner to Visit Indian Tribes in Kansas," *ibid.;* Sac and Fox Agency to Joseph Bogy *et al.,* January 9, 1867, Old Neosho Agency Records, Federal Records Center, Fort Worth; Concurrent Resolution of Kansas Legislature, February 5, 1868, 40A-H 8.2, RHR, RG 233, NA; John Mackintosh to J. Cox, March 18, 1870, LR-OIA, RG 75, M 234, R 690, F 0247–0251, NA; C. Delano to H. Dawes, January 12, 1871, SCLS-ID, ID, RG 48, M 606, R 10, F 97, NA; Vincent Colyer to Felix Brunot, April 13, 1870, Letters Received, Board of Indian Commissioners, RG 75, NA.

3. R. G. Ross to Secretary of Interior, September 8, 1871, LR-ID, ID, RG 48, M 825, R 26, F 0781, NA; Thomas Murphy to N. G. Taylor, February 8, 1869, LR-OIA, RG 75, M 234, R 738, F 0215, Sac and Fox Agency, NA; E. Hoag to

E. S. Parker, December 1, 1869, *ibid.;* T. E. Newlin to E. A. Hayt, March 15, 1878, Potawatomi Miscellaneous Correspondence, Federal Records Center, Kansas City; J. N. Morris to E. Hoag, January 20, 1871, LR-OIA, RG 75, M 234, R 690, F 0356–0357, Potawatomi Agency, NA; C. Delano to F. A. Walker, March 16, 1872, *ibid.,* R 691, F 0103–0104; J. Pratt to T. Murphy, February 6, 1868, LR-OIA, RG 75, M 234, R 279, F 0244–0249, Delaware Agency, NA; Fall Leaf to Department of Interior, February 3, 1867, *ibid.,* R 276, F 0974.

4. G. C. Snow to Thomas Murphy, March 17, 1869, Old Neosho Agency, Federal Records Center, Fort Worth; H. L. Taylor to Murphy, June 15, 1867, LR-OIA, RG 75, M 234, R 815, F 0264–0265, Shawnee Agency, NA; Sidney Clarke to N. G. Taylor, April 22, 1869, GIC-ID, ID, RG 48, Box 24, NA; Fall Leaf to William Dole, March 7, 1865, LR-OIA, RG 75, M 234, R 277, F 0086, Delaware Agency, NA; Albert Wiley to N. G. Taylor, January 12, 25, 1869, LR-OIA, RG 75, M 234, R 738, F 0208, Sac and Fox Agency, NA; W. Craig to E. Hoag, December 29, 1869, *ibid.,* F 0449; Edward Mc-Coom to Vincent Colyer, February 17, 1872, *ibid.,* R 739, F 0172; H. C. Linn to E. A. Hayt, February 3, 1879, Potawatomi Miscellaneous Correspondence, Federal Records Center, Kansas City; A. Wiley to T. Murphy, February 9, 1869, W. Craig to Murphy, April 13, 1869, A. C. Farnham to N. G. Taylor, March 11, 1869, LR-OIA, RG 75, M 234, R 738, F 0270, 0248, 0247, Sac and Fox Agency, NA.

5. G. Snow to T. Murphy, October 8, 1867, GIC-ID, ID, RG 58, Box 22, NA; *ibid.,* June 24, 1868, Box 21; Snow to Murphy, October 3, 1868, Osage Administration Miscellaneous Records, Box 415040, Federal Records Center, Fort Worth.

6. J. Garrett to V. Colyer, February 8, 1870, Letters Received, Board of Indian Commissioners, RG 75, NA; Tatham to Colyer, June 29, 1870, *ibid.;* ? to Colyer, July 19, 1870, *ibid.;* Board of Indian Commissioners, Minutes, July 27, 1870, *ibid.;* Colyer to C. Delano, January 24, 1871, Letters Sent, Board of Indian Commissioners, RG 75, NA; John Lang to Colyer, January 28, 1871, Letters Received, Board of Indian Commissioners, RG 75, NA.

7. John Rydjord, *Indian Place–Names* (Norman, 1968).

8. *Premium List, Rules and Regulations and Program. Pota-*

watomie Indian Fair Ass'n., Sept. 18–20, 1905 (St. Marys, 1905), vol. 7, Indian Pamphlets Collection, Kansas State Historical Society; Uriah Spray to C. Beede, December 5, 1876, Osage Administration Miscellaneous Records, Box 415040, Federal Records Center, Fort Worth; John Farwell to Board of Indian Commissioners, February 13, 1871, Letters Received, Board of Indian Commissioners, RG 75, NA.

Bibliography

ARCHIVAL MATERIAL: THE NATIONAL ARCHIVES,
WASHINGTON, D. C.

RG 46   Records of the United States Senate, President's Mes-
         ages, Indian Relations, 1854–1871.
RG 48   General Incoming Correspondence, Indian Division,
         Interior Department, 1854–1871.
RG 48   M 606   Special Classes of Letters Sent, Indian
         Division, Interior Department, 1854–1871.
         Lands and Railroads Division, Interior Depart-
         ment.
RG 48   M 825   Letters Received (Miscellaneous), Indian
         Division, Interior Department, 1854–1871.
RG 75   Letters Received, Records of the Board of Indian
         Commissioners, 5 vols., 1870–1873.
RG 75   Special Case Files, 1854–1871.
RG 75   M 234   Letters Received by the Office of Indian
         Affairs:
         Central Superintendency, 1854–1872 (R 55–62).
         Delaware Agency, 1855–1873 (R 274–280).
         Kansas Agency, 1854–1871 (R 364–368).
         Kickapoo Agency, 1855–1871 (R 371–373).
         Neosho Agency, 1852–1873 (R 531–536).
         New York Agency, 1852–1873 (R 588–591).
         Osage Agency, 1847–1874 (R 633).

Osage River Agency, 1855–1871 (R 645–651).
Ottawa Agency, 1863–1873 (R 656–658).
Potawatomi Agency, 1854–1871 (R 679–690).
Sac and Fox Agency, 1851–1873 (R 733–739).
Shawnee Agency, 1855–1871 (R 809–819).
RG 233   Records of the United States House of Representatives, 1854–1871.

ARCHIVAL MATERIAL: FEDERAL RECORDS CENTER
Fort Worth, Texas:
Old Neosho Correspondence, Box 415040, 1860–1877.
Osage Agency Records.
Kansas City, Missouri:
Potawatomi Miscellaneous Correspondence, Books 1 and 6, 1870–1876.

GOVERNMENT DOCUMENTS AND PUBLICATIONS
Annual Reports of the Commissioner of Indian Affairs, 1854–1871.
Congressional Globe.
Kappler, Charles J. *Indian Affairs. Laws and Treaties.* Vol. II, *Treaties,* Washington, Government Printing Office, 1904.
Letter from the Secretary of the Interior Transmitting Reports in Reference to the Carrying Out of the Treaty Stipulations with the Delaware Indians, February 3, 1855. *House Executive Document No. 50,* 33d Cong., 2d Sess. (Serial 783).
Report of the Secretary of War in Compliance with a Resolution Calling for Correspondence Relative to the Military Reservation at Fort Leavenworth, February, 1855. *Senate Executive Document No. 50,* 33d Cong., 2d Sess. (Serial 752).
Senate Report No. 4240, February 2, 1905. 58th Cong., 3d Sess. (Serial 4756).
U.S. Statutes at Large.

NEWSPAPERS
Arkansas Gazette (Little Rock).
Freedom's Champion (Atchison, Kansas).
Humboldt Union (Humboldt, Kansas).
Junction City Western Union (Junction City, Kansas).
Kansas Daily Tribune (Lawrence).

Kansas Weekly Herald (Leavenworth).
Leavenworth Daily Conservative (Leavenworth).
Missouri Democrat (St. Louis).
National Intelligencer (Washington, D.C.).
New York Times (New York).
Ottawa Journal (Ottawa, Kansas).
Sedalia Weekly Democrat (Sedalia, Missouri).
Smoky Hill and Republican Union (Junction City, Kansas).
The Kansas Chief (White Cloud, Kansas).
Topeka State Record (Topeka, Kansas).
Vinita Chieftain (Vinita, Indian Territory).
Western Journal of Commerce (Kansas City).
Wyandotte Gazette (Wyandotte, Kansas).

MANUSCRIPT COLLECTIONS

Leavenworth, Lawrence & Galveston Railroad Papers, Burlington Archives, Newberry Library, Chicago.

Sidney Clarke Papers, Federal Records Center, Fort Worth, Texas

George Crawford Papers, Department of Special Collections, Ablah Library, Wichita State University, Wichita, Kansas.

PAMPHLETS

Indian Pamphlets, Library Division, Kansas State Historical Society.

Indian Pamphlets, Frank Phillips Collection, University of Oklahoma Library.

Tauy Jones House, Early Meeting Place of the Free Staters. Franklin County Pamphlet, Library Division, Kansas State Historical Society.

Thacher, S. O. *Brief and Argument for Appelant, The United States of America vs. Leavenworth, Lawrence, and Galveston Railroad,* Circuit Court of the United States District of Kansas, n. d., Indian Pamphlet, Vol. 6, Library Division, Kansas State Historical Society.

———. *Reply to Briefs of Counsel for Complainant, The United States of America vs. Leavenworth, Lawrence, and Galveston Railroad,* Circuit Court of the United District Court of Kansas, n.d., Indian Pamphlet, Vol. 6, Library Division, Kansas State Historical Society.

BOOKS

Andreas, A. T. *History of the State of Kansas.* Chicago, A. T. Andreas, 1883.

Connelley, William E. *A Standard History of Kansas and Kansans.* Chicago, The American Historical Society, Inc., 1928. 5 vols.

Deloria, Vine, Jr. *Custer Died for Your Sins: An Indian Manifesto.* New York, Avon Books, 1970.

Elkins, Stanley. *Slavery: A Problem in American Institutional and Intellectual Life.* Chicago, University of Chicago Press, 1959.

Emmons, David. *Garden in the Grassland: Boomer Literature of the Central Great Plains.* Lincoln, University of Nebraska Press, 1971.

Gaeddert, G. Raymond. *The Birth of Kansas.* Lawrence, The University of Kansas, 1940.

Gates, Paul Wallace. *Fifty Million Acres: Conflicts over Kansas Land Policy, 1854–1890.* New York, Atherton Press, 1966.

Gibson, A. M. *The Kickapoos: Lords of the Middle Border.* Norman, University of Oklahoma Press, 1963.

Hagan, William T. *The Sac and Fox Indians.* Norman, University of Oklahoma Press, 1958.

Hill, Edward E. *The Office of Indian Affairs: Historical Sketches.* New York, Clearwater Press, 1974.

Holloway, J. N. *History of Kansas: From the First Exploration of the Mississippi Valley, to its Admission into the Union.* Lafayette, Indiana, James and Emmons, 1868.

Holmes, Oliver W. *The Common Law.* Boston, Little, Brown, and Co., 1881.

Hurst, James W. *Law and Economic Growth; the Legal History of the Lumber Industry in Wisconsin, 1836–1915.* Cambridge, Belknap Press of Harvard University Press, 1964.

Johnston, William. *Petition for Review before the Secretary of Interior on the Osage Purchase in Kansas vs. Railroad Companys.* Washington, Judd and Detweiler, 1870.

Jordan, Winthrop. *White over Black: American Attitudes Toward the Negro, 1550–1812.* Chapel Hill, University of North Carolina Press, 1968.

Landes, Ruth. *The Prairie Potawatomi.* Madison, The University of Wisconsin Press, 1970.

McCloskey, Robert. *American Conservatism in the Age of Enterprise: A Study of William Graham Sumner, Stephen J. Field, and Andrew Carnegie.* Cambridge, Harvard University Press, 1951.

Malin, James C. *Indian Policy and Western Expansion. Bulletin of the University of Kansas, Humanistic Studies,* II, No. 3, Lawrence, The University of Kansas, 1921.

——. *The Nebraska Question, 1852–1854.* Lawrence, The Author, 1953.

Marberry, M. M. *The Golden Voice, A Biography of Isaac Kalloch.* New York, Farrar, Straus, and Co., 1947.

Marx, Leo. *The Machine in the Garden.* New York, Oxford University Press, 1967.

Masterson, V. V. *The Katy Railroad and the Last Frontier.* Norman, University of Oklahoma Press, 1952.

Miner, H. Craig. *The Corporation and The Indian: Tribal Sovereignty and Industrial Civilization in Indian Territory, 1865–1907.* Columbia, University of Missouri Press, 1976.

Möllhausen, Baldwin. *Diary of a Journey from the Mississippi to the Coast of the Pacific.* London, Longman, Brown, Green, Longmans, and Roberts, 1858. 2 vols.

Moore, Barrington. *Social Origins of Dictatorship and Democracy: Lord and Peasant in the Modern World.* Boston, Beacon Press, 1966.

Nash, Roderick. *Wilderness and the American Mind.* New Haven, Yale University Press, 1967.

Nichols, Roy F. *The Disruption of American Democracy.* New York, Macmillan Publishing Co., Inc., 1948.

Parrish, William E. *David Rice Atchison of Missouri, Border Politician.* Columbia, University of Missouri Press, 1961.

Phillips, William. *The Conquest of Kansas, by Missouri and Her Allies.* Boston, Phillips, Sampson, and Company, 1856.

Robinson, Charles. *The Kansas Conflict.* Lawrence, Journal Publishing Co., 1898.

Rydjord, John. *Indian Place–Names; Their Origin, Evolution, and Meaning, Collected in Kansas in Siouan, Algonkian, Shoshonian, Caddoan, Iroquoian and other Tongues.* Norman, University of Oklahoma Press, 1968.

Schultz, George A. *An Indian Canaan, Isaac McCoy and the Vision of an Indian State.* Norman, University of Oklahoma Press, 1972.

Tuttle, Charles R. *A New Centennial History of the State of Kansas.* Madison, Inter-state Book Co., 1876.

Unrau, William E. *The Kansa Indians: A History of the Wind People, 1673–1873.* Norman, University of Oklahoma Press, 1971.

———. *The Kaw People.* Phoenix, Indian Tribal Series, 1975.

Weslager, C. A. *The Delaware Indians.* New Brunswick, Rutgers University Press, 1972.

ARTICLES AND ESSAYS

Abel, Annie H. "Indian Reservations in Kansas and the Extinguishment of Their Title," *Transactions of the Kansas State Historical Society,* VII (1904).

Berkhofer, Robert F., Jr. "The Political Context of a New Indian History," *Pacific Historical Review,* XL, No. 3 (August, 1971).

Chapman, Berlin B. "Removal of the Osages from Kansas," *Kansas Historical Quarterly,* VII, Nos. 3 and 4 (August, 1938, and November, 1938).

Danziger, Edmund, Jr. "The Office of Indian Affairs and Problem of Civil War Refugees in Kansas," *Kansas Historical Quarterly,* XXXV, No. 3 (Autumn, 1969).

Ferris, Ida M. "The Sauks and Foxes in Franklin and Osage Counties," *Collections of the Kansas State Historical Society,* XI (1910).

Gates, Paul Wallace. "A Fragment of Kansas Land History: The Disposal of the Christian Indian Tract," *Kansas Historical Quarterly,* VI, No. 3 (August, 1937).

———. "Indian Allotments Preceding the Dawes Act," in John Clark, ed., *The Frontier Challenge: Responses to the Trans-Mississippi West* (Lawrence, University Press of Kansas, 1971).

"Governor Reeder's Administration," *Transactions of the Kansas State Historical Society,* V (1889–1896).

Gowing, Clara. "Life Among the Delaware Indians," *Collections of the Kansas State Historical Society,* XII (1911–1912).

Le Duc, Thomas. "History and Appraisal of U. S. Land Policy in 1862," in Allan Bogue, Thomas Phillips, and James Wright, eds., *The West of the American People* (Itasca, F. E. Peacock, Inc., 1970).

Metcalf, P. Richard. "Who Shall Rule at Home? Native American Politics and Indian-White Relations," *The Journal of American History*, LXI, No. 3 (December, 1974).

Meyer, Roy W. "The Iowa Indians, 1836–1855," *Kansas Historical Quarterly*, XXVIII, No. 3 (Autumn, 1962).

Miner, H. Craig. "Border Frontier: The Missouri River, Fort Scott & Gulf Railroad in the Cherokee Neutral Lands, 1868–1870," *Kansas Historical Quarterly*, XXXV, No. 2 (Summer, 1969).

Nicholson, William. "A Tour of Indian Agencies and Indian Territory in 1870," *Kansas Historical Quarterly*, III, No. 3 (August, 1934).

Socolofsky, Homer E. "Wyandot Floats," *Kansas Historical Quarterly*, XXXVI, No. 3 (Autumn, 1970).

Taylor, David G. "Boom Town Leavenworth: The Failure of a Dream," *Kansas Historical Quarterly*, XXXVIII, No. 4 (Winter, 1972).

Unrau, William E. "The Civilian as Indian Agent: Villain or Victim?," *Western Historical Quarterly*, III, No. 4 (October, 1972).

UNPUBLISHED THESES AND DISSERTATIONS

Miner, H. Craig. "The Border Tier Line: A History of the Missouri River, Fort Scott, and Gulf Railroad, 1865–1870," M.A., History Department, Wichita State University, 1967.

Murphy, Joseph Francis. "Potawatomi Indians of the West: Origins of the Citizens Band," Ph.D., History Department, University of Oklahoma, 1961.

Index

Index   *175*

Osage treaty of 1865, 27, 98, 121; Potawatomi treaty of 1861, 29, 30–31, 40, 44–45, 84, 85, 87; Sac and Fox treaty, 5, 27, 77, 103; Shawnee treaty, 5, 19, 27, 91–92, 93; Sturgis treaty of 1868, 121, 122, 123, 124–125, 126

Indian tribes: Cherokee, 31, 117, 118, 126, 136; Choctaw, 30, 31; Delaware, 3, 29, 32, 33–43, 65–68, 80, 109–112, 113, 114, 115, 136; Kansa, 3, 6, 17, 78, 101–102, 141; Kickapoo, 3, 20, 45–49, 58–59, 96–98, 133–134, 139; Miami, 3, 16, 18, 19, 24, 100, 120–121; Osage, 3, 6, 31–32, 45, 98–99, 121–122, 123–132, 138–139; Ottawa, 3, 67–68; Pawnee, 6, 136; Potawatomi, 3, 18, 20, 32, 43–45, 51, 70–71, 73, 82–91, 102, 133, 135–136, 139, 141; Sac-Fox, 3, 20, 45, 51, 61–63, 64, 73–74, 77–78, 102–105, 116, 135, 137, 139; Shawnee, 3, 16, 50–51, 71–72, 74, 91–95, 116, 134; Wyandot, 3, 7

Irwin, M. Howard, 33
Isaacs, Andrew J., 24, 35, 72

James, Burton A., 20, 63, 64–65, 70
Johnson, Fielding, 40, 65–67
Johnson, S. W., 24
Johnston, William, 128–129
Journeycake, Charles, 37
Joy, James F., 117–118, 119, 121, 122, 123, 125, 126, 129

Kansa Indians, 3, 6, 17, 78, 101–102, 141
Kansas Central railroad, 33
Kansas Nebraska Bill, 5, 11, 12, 13
Kansas & Neosho Valley railroad, 116–117. See also Missouri River, Fort Scott & Gulf railroad

Kansas and the Osage Swindle, 124–125
Keith, Charles, 47, 48–49, 58, 59, 96, 97
Keokuk, 102–103
Keokuk, Moses, 7, 61–62, 63, 66, 78, 103, 104–106, 135
Keoquark, 97
Kickapoo Indians, 3, 20, 45–49, 58–59, 96–98, 133–134, 139
Kickapoo treaty of 1862, 29, 30–31, 47, 48–49, 58–59, 96, 98
King, Matthew, 75
Kis-ke-to-no, 20
Knapp, E. N., 48

Lane, Senator James, 36, 38, 40, 75
Lawler, Thomas, 59
Lawrence, William, 122, 127, 128
Lea, Luke, 63
Leavenworth, 13–16, 42, 108–114, 129
Leavenworth, Lawrence & Galveston railroad, 31, 98, 121–131, 138
Leavenworth, Pawnee & Western railroad, 28, 29, 31, 32, 33, 35, 36, 40, 82–83, 85, 98. *See also* Union Pacific, Eastern Division railroad
Le Duc, Thomas, 52
Lincoln, President Abraham, 19, 28, 34
Lykins, Johnston, 8

Machine in the Garden, The, 25
Maclin, Sackfield, 110, 111
Manypenny, George, 8–17, 22–24, 52, 69–73, 91, 109, 110, 111–112, 116
Martin, Henry, 63, 105
Max, Leo, 25
McCaslin, Maxwell, 16, 18
McClelland, Robert, 13, 16
McCloskey, Robert, 26
McCoy, Reverend Isaac, 5

McCoy, John C., 13, 111
Meacham, James, 5, 11
Metcalf, P. Richard, 100–101
Miami Claim Association, 19
Miami Indians, 3, 16, 18, 19, 24,
100, 120–121
Missouri, Kansas & Texas railroad
company, 76, 125–130, 138. *See
also* Union Pacific, Southern
Branch
Missouri River, Fort Scott & Gulf
railroad, 117, 118, 121, 126, 131
Missouri River railroad, 29, 41
Mix, Charles, 104
Mo-ko-ho-ko, 63, 105, 135, 137
Möllhausen, Baldwin, 26
Moore, Ely, 24
Mormon Church, 84
Murphy, Thomas, 38, 41–43, 59,
88, 97, 116, 135, 136
Murphy, William E., 82–84
Mut-tut-tah, 103, 105

National Intelligencer, 110, 114
Navarre, Anthony, 84–88, 90–91,
100
Neosho valley, 9
Ne-graw-ho, 135
Ne-sour-quoit, 103–104
New England Emigrant Aid
Society, 16
Newsom, B. J., 92, 93–94
Nokowhat, 97

Ogden, E. A., 110, 111, 112
Osage Indians, 3, 6, 31–32, 45, 98–
99, 121–122, 123–132, 138–139
Osage treaty of 1865, 27, 98, 121
Osage valley, 9
Ottawa Indians, 3, 67–68
Ottawa Indian University, 67–68,
100

Pah-kah-hoh, 48
Palmer, Luther, 86, 87, 88, 89, 91

Parks, Chief Joseph, 71–72, 91,
93, 94, 95
Parks, Samuel, 50
Pawnee Indians, 6, 136
Paw-ne-no-pos-he, Joseph, 98–99
Peoria, Baptiste, 76
Perry, J. D., 38, 43-44
Pet-ti-quauk, 97, 98
Pierce, President Franklin, 14, 17,
18, 24
Pomeroy, Senator Samuel, 29, 36,
38, 39, 47–48, 57, 58, 66, 87, 96,
98, 127, 129
Potawatomi Indians, 3, 18, 20, 32,
43–45, 51, 70–71, 73, 82–91, 102,
133, 135–136, 139, 141
Potawatomi treaty of 1861, 29,
30–31, 40, 44–45, 84, 85, 87
Pratt, John, 38, 66
Preemption Law of 1841, 14, 119

Quantrill, William, 68
"Quindaro Brewery," 20

Reeder, Andrew H., 20–24, 71
Robideaux, John, 120–121
Robinson, Benjamin F., 13, 16
Robinson, Charles M., 16, 94
Ross, Potawatomi Indian agent,
85–86, 88, 89, 91
Rushmore, Alexander, 90

Sac-Fox Indians, 3, 20, 45, 51, 61–
63, 64, 73–74, 77–78, 102–105,
116, 135, 137, 139
Sac and Fox treaty, 5, 27, 77, 103
Sarcoxie, 16, 80, 99, 100
Sears, T. C., 130–131
Seward, William, 11
Shawnee Indians, 3, 16, 50–51, 71–
72, 74, 91–95, 116, 134
Shawnee treaty, 5, 19, 27, 91–92,
93
Sibley, George C., 101
Smith, Caleb B., 19
Snow, George C., 98, 138